From Our Doorsteps

Developing a Ministry Plan That Makes Sense

RICK MORSE

CHALICE PRESS

ST. LOUIS, MISSOURI

Cover art: Image Ideas, Inc.
Cover and interior design: Elizabeth Wright

Visit Chalice Press on the World Wide Web at
www.chalicepress.com

10 9 8 7 6 5 4 3 2 1   10   11   12   13   14   15

EPUB: 978-08272-10455   EPDF: 978-08272-10462

Library of Congress Cataloging-in-Publication Data
Morse, Rick.
  From our doorsteps : developing a ministry plan that makes sense / by Rick Morse.
    p. cm.
  ISBN 978-0-8272-1044-8
  1. Church work. 2. Communities–Religious aspects–Christianity. 3. Mission of the church. 4. Church. I. Title.

BV4400.M677 2010
254'.5–dc22

                                                          2010008564

Printed in United States of America

Contents

• *Extra information about researching your community is available on the* From Our Doorsteps *product page on www.ChalicePress.com.*

Foreword

I believe in the transforming power of Jesus Christ. I have seen the Christian story impact people's lives and bring wholeness and well-being for many. I also believe that God calls us to explore the Christian story together in faith communities. I believe it is impossible to investigate the scriptures and come to the conclusion that you can be spiritual without a faith community.

I have watched many dedicated ministers and laypeople over the past thirty years who have given their lives toward reaching others in their churches, only to be disappointed, confused, and finally even cynical. Despite these heroic efforts, congregations are failing at an alarming pace, with more than 50,000 churches closing in the past century and accelerating numbers of people who are unaffiliated with any faith community.

Congregational leaders have more resources, education, and outreach methods than any previous generation. Compared with congregations in the past, they have better facilities, far more funding and capital assets, and lots of books about how to do it better. Yet churches are struggling to pay bills and keep their doors open.

During the past eight years, it has been my privilege to work with hundreds of new and existing congregations who are trying to reach their communities. I find that people really know what the Bible says about hospitality, evangelism, and mission. I also find that they have the passion to reach out to others in meaningful ways. People are getting stuck, however, with interpreting our rapidly changing culture, our communities, and the realities of what a congregation can effectively achieve.

This is likely because congregations have used an old model for planning, namely the "problem solving" method, for generations. This linear approach has us fixing small things about our congregations without really doing anything to "adapt" to our changing environment. While Church Extension, the unit of the Christian Church (Disciples of Christ) where I serve, does not offer ministry-planning services, there is a large need for such a planning process. Therefore, I spent my sabbatical writing this book to fill that need.

In the past decades our culture has undergone a massive shift. However, many of our congregations are stuck in the glory days of the past. Leaders recognize the need to change, but they have not been able to initiate the kind of change needed. They have attended workshops, read books, and listened to engaging speakers, but when they get home they discover that what sounded good is met with resistance. That is largely because it is impossible to engage everyone in the same process at the same time.

This book turns most planning methods upside down. It enables congregational leaders to encounter the same process of discovery together by: (1) exploring the culture, (2) exegeting the community, (3) assessing the congregation's resources, and (4) rediscovering God's call for this context and time. At the end leaders can follow a process to develop a ministry plan so that they can lead the congregation in a similar journey of discovery together.

My desire and passion for writing this book stems out of my love of God. The Gospel has a profound ability to help ordinary people live extraordinary lives, and *congregations* make a huge impact on the lives of people who are engaged in them. There is no other transforming organism in the world like a vital congregation.

While this book attempts to measure many things, no process can ever truly measure the difference a church makes in people's lives. *The goal is for a congregation to make a difference, helping people grow in potential and courage in order to be the people God has truly called us to be.*

No book is big enough; neither workshops powerful enough; nor evangelism committees skillful enough to transform a church. It only happens when people journey together and discover what God is calling them to do. A powerful transformation takes place when congregations comprehend who they are and what God calls them to be. These transformed congregations find a different way of being church and begin to answer the very questions that people are asking. More simply put, vital congregations transform lives. They do so because people who have unleashed the power of the Gospel in their own lives cannot help but touch the lives of new people who come into contact with them.

I affirm this because at an early age a vital congregation transformed me and continues to transform me as I grow older. I am nowhere near the same person I would have been had it not been for the church and the way it has forced me to continually ask myself if my thoughts, behavior, and spirit honor God. The church has forced me to reconsider long held convictions, principles, and values, and has led me to a point in life where I can see the fruits of faithful living I desperately want that for others.

My heart breaks for the growing numbers of people who no longer find relevance in a faith community. I also become restless thinking about my colleagues in ministry who work so hard and are deeply dedicated to their congregations, but feel they cannot achieve their calling in the church as it is today.

This book is for those who want to make a difference, and for the millions who have yet to discover the transforming power of the Gospel when shared collectively.

Introduction

Earlier in my life I used to teach sailing. One summer week in the Puget Sound an acquaintance asked me if I would be willing to sail with him as his "safety net." He had been day sailing for a couple of years and was ready to begin cruising, but wanted me to go along "just in case." His instructions to me were clear: "Don't say anything until I am on the brink of trouble." I agreed; after all, an efficient boat can only have one skipper.

We loaded the boat and were ready to set off with his wife, son, and another couple. I was looking forward to a week without much responsibility and was eager to enjoy the sights and sounds of sailing in the Pacific Northwest.

As we cast off I asked the skipper where we were headed. His reply made me nervous: "north." I asked again, "You mean the North-Rim Islands?" to which he said…"yeah, ok." We left the dock with provisions, but not a destination.

Sailing in the Northwest requires some planning. You really need to be in a harbor by 3:30 in the afternoon or you may not find a spot to anchor for hours. You also have to be aware of the evening's weather report and find a harbor that is sheltered from the prevailing winds; otherwise you could have a miserable evening dragging and resetting anchors.

By 3:00 in the afternoon, our crew had sailed to the North Rim Islands, and I asked the skipper, "Have you decided where we are going to anchor tonight?" By his look of indecision, it was obvious he had not. He began to think out loud about places we could go and spotted a harbor nearby that was exposed to prevailing winds from the north. "Yeah…we'll spend the night at Matia."

Having listened to the weather report I was leery, but trying not to step on his toes I politely asked: "Did you listen to the weather report today? It stated that we are going to have winds tonight from the north at thirty knots." He quickly replied, "The weather man has been wrong all week. Besides, I can see with my own eyes that the dock there is wide open, and we can tie up directly instead of anchoring."

His wife was also growing concerned. She used her binoculars and looked off to the distance. "I can see a harbor on the south side of Patos Island. It looks clear." The skipper squinted trying to see for himself. "I've made up my mind. We are headed for Matia," he said.

After threading the rocks into the harbor of Matia we tied up. We enjoyed the evening, exploring the island, eating a big dinner, and watching a beautiful sunset. At 2:00 a.m., however, the trip turned sour.

Winds came barreling down on us from the north at thirty-five knots. Our boat was being smashed up against the dock, and there was chaos on board. The skipper sat up in his bunk with a look of surprise on his face. The wave action threw the rest of us on the floor. With no direction from the skipper, everyone started doing what they thought would be best.

I went out on the dock, lashed the wheel hard right, and tried to prevent the boat from sustaining any more damage. The couple started picking up dishes and food that had fallen from the cupboards and were cleaning up the cabin. The skipper was finally listening to the weather report. The skipper's wife took a super-sized sleeping pill.

Since it was very dark, we couldn't leave the port through the treacherous rocks. So we spent the evening sitting on the floor, playing cards, while getting hit in the head by the occasional falling object. Not exactly the "restful" vacation we had hoped for.

It is no surprise to me that the Greek word for "boat" in the New Testament is *oikome.* The same word is sometimes translated as "church." I believe our ancestors in the faith understood that the church is much like a boat. It is a vessel that takes a group of people, who are called for a particular purpose, on a journey to a place they never thought they could go.

Unfortunately, a "boat" is only good when it is going somewhere. A boat tied up to a dock is merely a "hole in the water where you throw money," as sailors like to say. The docks of any marina today are lined with dozens of boats that rarely get used. It is sad to see such wasted "journey potential."

Many of our churches today are boats tied to docks. The passengers on board are going nowhere with their faith journeys, and the crew continues to abandon ship. The common theme of what holds us back is our inability to cast a vision for our future heading.

In our sailing story, the skipper was leading without a sense of purpose or direction. He was just heading north. He earnestly rejected sound advice. He didn't even look through the binoculars his wife offered in order to consider another location. Instead, he steered the boat on the easiest course and took the easiest harbor (one rejected by other skippers that day). Then, when the storm hit, he watched his crew scurry in many different directions and did little to change the situation.

As church leaders, we want our churches to make a difference in people's lives with the Good News of Jesus Christ. This book is meant as a way of setting a new course for your congregation's future. This book will enable you to explore the future by gaining enough consensus from the congregation to make an intentional decision for your course.

Binoculars help a person see into the distance. They do not have just a single lens, but a combination of lenses and prisms that enable us to bring distant objects into closer perspective. Once the person looking through the binoculars has clarity about what lies ahead, he or she can chart a future course and encourage others to make the trip too.

If a person uses only a single lens, the object does not become appreciably larger, and appears upside down.[1]

Most congregations tend to look at their context for ministry with only one lens. Usually that lens is either a theological/biblical base for the church's existence, or just a cultural lens.

To be an effective church, we must look at our mission through numerous lenses, like binoculars. Binoculars make distant objects appear closer and undistorted. Keeping with our sailing metaphor, every good skipper has a set of binoculars to make good decisions about the vessel's future path.

We will be looking toward your congregation's future through a number of lens and prisms. The first lens (the "objective" lens) will provide a macro view of your context. We will explore postmodernity and the major shift in cultural values we are now experiencing.

The second and third sections are like prisms, since they are reflective of the current specific situation in which you are doing ministry. We will discuss how your church can evaluate its community

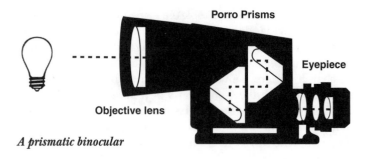

A prismatic binocular

and come to grips with the demographic gaps the church may be experiencing. We will also spend time assessing your congregation's strengths, resources, and passion.

As the image becomes clearer, we will focus our eyepiece on the following question: How does the Bible guide us in choosing our vision? The final section will then center on how to write a "Ministry Plan."

When we look at our context through *all* of these lenses and prisms, a new image appears, and our imagination can begin to explore a new future for our congregation.

This book is designed to be studied by groups of leaders in your church as a practical guide toward seeking a new future. My hope is that you will find a way to "untie" your church from indecision so you can lead the congregation on the journey that God intends you to take.

Is It Worth Leaving the Dock?

Let me finish the previous sailing yarn about our stormy night at Matia. At first light we left the dock in a thirty-five–knot gale. It was difficult navigating out of the rocky cove. It took lookouts from the crew to provide mid-course corrections to navigate the current, wind, and waves. Once we got to a point where we could raise our sails, we left the stormy cove and very quickly found a new place to explore.

When congregations are vital, they are a thing of wonder. I don't think there is any organization as effective and meaningful for people's lives as the church when it is fully functioning and full of God's spirit. It is the only organization that helps people of every generation grow spiritually and developmentally. While schools do effective jobs with a generation, the church works with every generation. While businesses motivate their employees to work hard with a salary, it is nothing like the scores of volunteers who do worthwhile things in their communities and even abroad for little or no remuneration so as to fulfill the Great Commission.

Consider what a church does for younger children developmentally. When a child is dedicated in a church, the parents begin to sense that their child is a gift from God and a person to be treated with great respect. The church community accepts children and treats them like their own. They become adopted aunts and uncles, grandmas and grandpas for a child who may be growing up far from extended family.

Consider what a church does for children in early childhood. They learn about the Creator and begin to sense that they are not the center of the universe. They explore the world with wonder, learning that God is reaching out to them to be their friend. Children who learn to love God have great socialization skills compared with children who do not experience the church in this way.

Consider what a vital congregation can do for teens going through the identity issues of adolescence. When they are part of a church youth group, they see themselves more clearly through the eyes of other Christian youth. They separate from their nuclear family, developing meaningful relationships as they work together on mission trips and other events. They learn at an early age that they can contribute to the life of the church in meaningful ways and that their gifts might be different from others. This is very different from the pressure they receive from classmates to conform to certain standards and not trust the "establishment."

Consider what a vital congregation can do for young adults. Many young adults have moved to a new community and are beginning their first career. Churches provide places where they can establish new relationships, find meaning in life, and discover new recreational opportunities with groups of people whose sense of community is not based on spending lots of money or drinking a lot of beer. Young adults in these congregations report a higher level of happiness than their unchurched counterparts.

Consider what a vital congregation can do for newlyweds. They work with young couples in their rough early years. An elder of a congregation in Memphis was speaking about a coworker's father not long ago. This elder stated that the father had had ten children, and that he knew he would need the church to help him raise them. All of his children became ministers, social workers, police officers and loving parents themselves, largely because of the congregation that helped raise those children.

Consider what vital churches do for adults in their middle years with opportunities to grow together. Think about the ways in which adults in the same stage of life share information about doctors, the disease of the month that the kids are bringing home, or where to find good deals on clothing. It was great to also have time during the hectic week to pause and reflect. One single mother of five children once asked me if our time of silent prayer couldn't be just a bit longer. The silence meant so much to her, as it was the only quiet time she experienced the whole week.

And as we enter old age, the church makes remarkable contributions to our lives. For some in late retirement, the church is the only social contact they have during the week in which they see young children, teens, and adults all at the same time. Those personal connections make a huge difference in their lives.

My friend John Bristow once told me of a study he read that was completed by Kaiser Hospitals in Oregon. The study showed that hospitalized patients who claimed to be spiritual had shorter hospitalizations than those who claimed no spirituality. The same study also showed that those who claimed spirituality and were connected with a faith community had shorter hospitalizations than those who claimed spirituality, but were not a part of a faith community.

Vital congregations enable people to contemplate their own mortality, considering what kind of legacy they wish to leave others about a life well lived.

Finally, when a person faces life's final hours and a family is in crisis as they face the death of a loved one, the church is there to remind them that even though they walk in the shadow of death, they have nothing to fear. I have witnessed many remarkable times with families as they say good-bye to a loved one, and I also have personally felt the tremendous love and support from my faith community in the death of a loved one. I seriously don't know how people who are not a part of a faith community face those difficult times without that kind of support.

William Sloane Coffin, who was one of the greatest preachers, said:

> Miracles do not a messiah make. But a messiah can do miracles. If you ask me if Jesus literally raised Lazarus from the dead, literally walked on water or changed water into wine, I will answer "For certain I do not know."

BUT this I DO know: Faith must be lived before it is understood, and the more it is lived, the more things become possible.

I can also report that in home after home I have seen Jesus change beer into furniture, sinners into saints, hate-filled relationships into loving ones, cowardice into courage, the fatigue of despair into the buoyancy of hope. In instance after instance, life after life, I have seen Christ be "God's power unto salvation", and that is miracle enough for me![2]

The church is the place where people practice living faith *together*. You cannot read the scriptures and see that God has called us to be hermits, doing spiritual practices alone. Instead churches call us to bind ourselves to each other toward being instruments of God's peace in this world. The biblical record gives little indication that God's *shalom* (peace) is meant for our own personal satisfaction. Peace will never be realized until all creation enjoys it.

When you look at our nation's history, you can see that churches started the first hospitals. Churches started the first libraries. Mental health care began in churches. Public education is a by-product of churches. The very first European immigrants organized government in the first church building in North America.

Anthropologists will tell you that humans lived together in groups long before any written history. By living in groups or tribes, we became far more effective in helping each person in the group reach maturity, thus strengthening us to live in the world.

When congregations are at their best, members strengthen one another to stand against the injustices of our time. Together they find the courage to stand against racism and other inequalities experienced by people of all walks of life. Together they stand for those in the bottom rungs of our social structures and see to it that the hungry are fed, clothed, and sheltered. Any congregation can be that kind of place today.

One final thing about the Greek language: The word *pneuma* is the word for spirit as well as wind. It is ironic that God's breath or spirit is that which *propels* the boat or church.

God's wind is ever present, even though we cannot see it. There are some signs, like ripples on the water, of the divine presence, but the wind itself cannot be seen. The same is true for how God's spirit works in our congregations. We see signs of its presence in the people and in the small miracles we witness, even though the Spirit itself is invisible.

As church leaders we believe the wind of the spirit exists, and as a result we must set the sails, untie the boat from the dock, and take the people on a journey to a place they never thought they could go. I believe God gives us what we need to make the journey, but we must look to the future and focus our vision to find that place where God is leading us.

Questions for Discussion

1. Reflect on your entire experience in our congregation. Do you remember a time when you felt the most engaged, alive, and motivated? Who was involved? How did it feel?[3]
2. When you consider all of your experiences at our church, what has contributed most to your *spiritual life*?[4]
3. When you consider your entire life, was there a time when you feel the church helped you the most? What stage of life were you in? How did it help?
4. How far into the future is our congregation looking?
   a. ten years
   b. five years
   c. one year
   d. three months
   e. next Sunday
   f. about fifteen minutes
4. Is our boat (our congregation) tied up at the dock, or are under full sail toward a common goal?

1

A Macro Lens of Doing Church Today

Conversations with Travelers

The kind of church I grew up in really no longer exists because times have changed. People who can remember the church of the 50s and 60s know exactly what I am talking about. The world around us is significantly different.

In this chapter we will look through the first lens in our binoculars. The first lens is a large one called the "objective" lens. It is concave in shape, and takes in a large view before narrowing the focus of the object being looked at.[1]

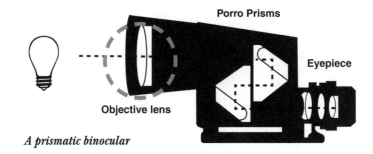

A prismatic binocular

To understand our context for ministry, we have to look at the big picture first. Understanding the cultural shifts enables us to see how the broader culture is impacting our community. To do this, we will meet three persons who will introduce us to the mind-set of the postmodern world today.

I travel a lot, and I love to visit with people. While I am most at ease talking with church people, I find it fascinating to visit with those who are not at all a part of the church culture. When you travel, you have time to visit with people, and when they are belted into a seat next to you...let's just say you have a "captive audience."

Priorities, Commitments, and Kids

My first seatmate on a plane was an architect who was working on a large stadium in my home city, Indianapolis. She was probably in her mid to late 30s. After a lengthy conversation about our new stadium she asked what I did for a living. When she discovered I was a minister, she made a statement that I hear over and over these days: "I am a spiritual person. I just don't think I have to be a part of organized religion."

I have learned over the years that this statement to a minister means, "Don't you dare try to talk me into coming to your church." But the statement goes a lot deeper than that. Fifty years ago, there was no question that spiritual people participated in congregations. Today that assumption does not exist. In fact, it is just the opposite. People of younger generations have grown up in a period where every kind of leader, including religious leaders, has earned their distrust.

My seatmate gave me a lot of insight into this mind-set when she talked about her family and their schedule. She juggles two small children who are engaged in every sport imaginable. Her husband also has a demanding profession in the building industry. He doesn't travel, but works twelve-hour days. When she travels, you can only imagine the logistical nightmare she has to organize, usually on short notice, before she leaves.

This woman is not atypical of many people today. Let's unpack her life for a moment to see what she is really saying.

Most Americans today see themselves as spiritual: 91 percent of households own a Bible; 80 percent of adults name the Bible as the most influential book in human history; and 96 percent of adults believe in God.[2] Yet despite those rousing numbers, only 49 percent of adults claim adherence to any faith community.[3]

David Olson did some excellent work on trying to measure the Sunday engagement of our population and found some startling results. In his research he took the average worship attendance of every denomination, added in estimates when they only had membership figures, and using consistent methods, measured church attendance over a fourteen-year period. The results were shocking: *almost all Christian groups are losing ground.* On any given Sunday in 1990, 20.4 percent of the population would be in church. Just fourteen yearls later that percentage had dropped to 17.7 percent.[4] Worse yet, Olson demonstrates a gain in the U.S. population of 53 million people since the 1980s. Yet Sunday morning worship attendance has remained constant. Simply put, there are many more people, and they are not attending church.[5]

This woman I met on the plane is not an exception; she is an example of what is happening in our culture today. People are not making a connection between spirituality and participation in a faith group. She is a part of a growing group, given that in a January 2002 Gallup poll 33 percent of Americans say they are "spiritual but not religious."[6]

My seatmate also discussed her family life. Few churches have taken into consideration the changes in the family over the past fifty years. In their surge for more productivity, businesses are getting more and more hours out of the typical worker. According to the U.S. Department of Labor, Americans are working more hours in a typical week than they did in 1976. In 1976, 23 percent of the workforce worked more than forty hours per week. Today that number is closer to 30 percent and the rate is growing despite higher unemployment. What is startling is this figure does not reflect those who are working more than one job.

When compared with the rest of the world, the average U.S. worker puts in 1,792 hours per year, while in Germany the average worker puts in only 1,432 hours annually.[7] This is a condition that we must recognize as congregations plan their programs. Churches can no longer expect to run a traditional schedule and meet the needs of people today. We can no longer expect multiple trips back and forth to a congregation for numerous events.

Since the 1950s the number of women in the workforce has nearly doubled. I happen to be the proud son of a mother who excelled in the workforce long before it was popular. I'm not saying it is good or bad; I am simply naming this change in conditions.

In the 1960s, the church had a wealth of volunteer labor, which came from a sense of duty but also from large numbers of women whose tremendous skills in management were not being used in the workforce.

Today, with nearly 80 percent of women working outside the home, that vital resource is missing. The churches that have not adapted to this new reality are hurting.

It has been widely recognized over the past couple of decades that when it comes to making a decision about which church a family will attend, the mother of a traditional family most often has the greatest influence on that decision. The choice may also include "not" attending any congregation. If demanding family and work patterns stress the person making this decision, the choice to cut back on or drop church attendance seems likely.

Another factor, one we cannot quantify, is the changing patterns of play with children. Most of us who are older remember our childhoods of many hours of unsupervised activities. That is to say, I had about a five-mile radius as a child, and I could ride my bike, explore, hike, and hang out with my friends as long as I was home by dinner. Today, with what we know about pedophiles and others who prey on children, our children are far less likely to have that kind of unsupervised freedom.

The cost of that has been that parents today have their young children in more supervised activities, which usually require a trip in the mini-van by a parent. The children may be in daycare (if they live in suburbia), or childcare (if they are metropolitan kids), or even latch-keyed (if they are underprivileged).

This dynamic also has led to children watching far more television than previous generations. Today the average youth spends 900 hours per year in school and an average of 1,500 hours watching television.[8]

Parents also spend more time in traffic. Today one in eight commuters leave home before 6:00 a.m., and that number is growing.[9] In some metropolitan areas a person will spend about six days' worth of time commuting to and from work each year.[10]

My traveling partner and her husband had worked 132 hours that week in stressful, demanding jobs. They spent lots of time in traffic. She ran at least five or six trips in the mini-van with her children to supervised activities, not to mention the chores of running a household and caring for their property. Time is valuable to this family, and their time must be spent in quality activities that they value.

Moving in the Global Economy

On another trip, I sat by a man in his 40s who was on his way for a job interview in another city. He had been in his current position for seven years and had hoped to stay longer, but the market was drying up and his company was starting to downsize. He could see the writing on the wall and wanted to get a new position in place before the "hammer fell."

He was clear with me that such a move was pretty disruptive, given his desire to stay in one place with his family. His wife would have to change teaching positions to a new school district, which would mean a loss for her retirement. However, the employment opportunities in his community would require him to take a substantial cut in pay, which the family could not afford. "We've moved a few times before; we'll do it again," he said.

This fellow traveler also said he was spiritual but not a part of organized religion.

This man demonstrated another example of what is happening to churches today. Mobility rates are climbing. My childhood church was filled with people who had worked for their company twenty or thirty years. Most of these adults were working for the same company they had worked for since they got out of the military after World War II.

That is not the case today. The average tenure for jobs in 1998 was 13.4 years.[11] Today that tenure rate is even lower, forcing increased mobility among families. In one community in which I served as a pastor, the mobility rate was 20 percent, which meant that each year one in five families would leave my community (and new ones would replace them).

This dynamic has had a big impact on congregations. Before 1950 we used to depend on "biology" to enable our churches to grow and sustain themselves. Our communities were largely "closed" systems. People would grow up in that community, marry, work in the community's industry, and retire there. This would give them continuity in friendships, and that would include their relationship with their church.

Stephen Compton, a Methodist Conference Minister who works in congregational development, noted this dynamic of the past.[12] A group of people would come together and start a church. As they had children, the church would grow. When those children grew up and married, they had grandchildren and spouses, adding to their numbers. Occasionally a newcomer would come to town to put down

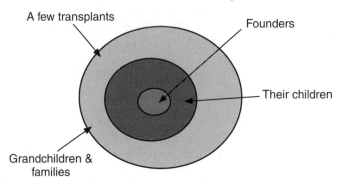

roots. This "closed" system worked for our congregations for many years, but depended on a much longer worker tenure rate.

Today people charter a congregation, and then seven years later they move. If they are lucky to remain in the community, when their children grow up those young adults leave home for employment opportunities somewhere else. And when they relocate, they usually become a part of that rapidly growing segment known as the unchurched.[13]

In addition our families are much smaller than they were in the 1960s. In that time (before birth control pills were widely used) the birth rate among American Anglos was 24 per 1,000 people. Today that number is just 11.[14] You cannot imagine the exponential impact of these dynamics over a fifty-year period.

Our population today is anything but stagnant. More than half of U.S. houses have been built since 1975.[15] Our population is becoming more urban as well. In 1960 about half of U.S. housing was in a rural or small town context. Today only 20 percent of U.S. housing is in that category. Employment opportunities in small communities for new people are few.

My seatmate explained what occurred to his former company: "Until 1990 our company was at the top of our game. I could call any of my leads and get an order on the same day. Then 1995 came, and we didn't get into the Internet for our marketing. We just thought personal service would mean something. Evidently price does. We were no longer competing with businesses in our state, but all over the country. Then, almost overnight, with the increased competition in air-freight, we were then competing with the whole world. We couldn't keep up."

Thomas Friedman's book *The World is Flat*[16] has provided tremendous insight into what is happening globally with the people in the communities we serve. He makes the point that you can no longer be a B+ college graduate in Indiana and compete in today's job market, because you are competing with people from around the world for the same job. Friedman cites the State of Indiana's employment office, which interested me because my office in downtown Indianapolis shares a building with it.

In 1995 the State of Indiana put out a bid for contracts for a software developer who was willing to rewrite their system for supporting out-of-work Hoosiers.[17] The bid was posted on the state's Internet site. While companies in Indiana put their proposals together, a software company in India picked up the request and wrote the winning proposal. That explains to me why so many foreign nationals from India work in my building. They are "employed" writing software for "unemployed" Hoosiers. The irony is that unemployed software programmers from Indiana are receiving their unemployment checks from a system developed by software programmers from India.

When I asked my seatmate about his new employment opportunity, I discovered he was looking at a position offered by a multinational company that was based in Japan, which allows me to introduce another dynamic that has impacted our congregations, namely what is called *"Glocality."*

Today we have both a Global and Local reality in just about every community in North America. Missiologist Ed Stezer first penned the term "Glocal":

> One of the biggest cultural barriers we face is the emerging of "glocal" context. We use this term to refer to the convergence of the *glo*bal reality with the lo*cal* reality. North America has become a "glocal community" requiring new strategies for effective ministry.[18]

It is rare in many coastal communities to not live near a first-generation immigrant family, or a foreign national who is working in the United States. This is changing our communities dramatically and is having a large impact on congregations that do not recognize this new reality.

Consider these statistics:

- Over the next fifty years the U.S. population will grow by 50 percent, and 90 percent of that growth will be people of color.

- In 2000, Hispanics became the largest racial ethnic minority in the United States.
- The United States today has the third largest Spanish speaking population in the world.
- By 2050 there will be no majority racial group.[19]

Already five states have no racial majority group, and the U.S. Census Bureau has adjusted its predictions to say that by 2042 there will be no majority racial group in America.[20] This change is happening very quickly.

Consider the dynamics of Los Angeles, where there is no majority population. It is a wonderful place to visit because it teems with so much cultural diversity. There is literally some sort of celebration every day. You can taste many new kinds of food. There are multinational corporations with foreign workers mixed in the population. And the congregations who are finding their multicultural voice are flourishing, while those who do not continue to decline.

Meanwhile, this second seatmate was on his way to a new life in a new city. He was not even thinking about whether there would be a new church for him and his family.

Young Adults Teach us about the Future

My last seatmate was a young man in his early 20s heading home for Thanksgiving vacation from his college in Arizona. I love meeting with young adults, and found this person fascinating. He was getting a degree in construction management, had completed a study abroad in Central America building housing for hurricane victims, and was looking forward to graduation that spring. He was an organizer who could get people to work together and accomplish a goal. This is a skill that I often look for in recruiting new church planters, so we began to breach the barrier of talking about faith.

After the standard "I'm spiritual, but not religious" comment, he began to talk about his upbringing.

> "Our family went to church about twice a month. I was bored out of my head every time we went. The music was awful, the sermons made no sense to me, and the rituals seemed meaningless. My parents told me that if I would complete a church membership class, they would let me decide my own participation level in the church. I went to church every Saturday for several months, and again found it tedious and boring. I was glad to hear about volunteer opportunities,

and did mission trips with our youth group, and worked in the local food bank, but when I finished the class, I basically started sleeping in on Sunday mornings."

I thought I might find an open spot, so I asked, "Isn't there *anything* that you miss about being in church on a Sunday?" His quick reply was "No."

The Mainline church has done an incredibly poor job of retaining young people, even when they remain in our communities. Today more generations are alive than at any other time in our history.[21] Each of these generations has been formed by the events of its time, and this young man is representative of those who came of age in the year 2000.

He has a different set of principles guiding his life. The grid below demonstrates some of the principles guiding his life, compared with those of us in older generations:

Some Younger Generational Principles	Some Older Generational Principles
I will participate in things that have value for me.	I will do whatever helps the group, even if I don't get anything out of it.
It is important to be different, even from my peers, in beliefs, dress etc. Being an individual shows maturity	I appreciate that when I go to a national chain, it will be exactly the same no matter what. I dress similarly to my peers, and try not to rock the boat if my beliefs are different from those whom I am with.
I appreciate having a variety of choices of food, learning opportunities, and recreation.	I like a limited number of choices and am striving for stability.
Committees are a bogus waste of time. They accomplish so little after lots of talk. We should keep things loose.	Committees are how you get things done. You must have organization.
If we want to do something, we should do it now and figure out how to pay for it later.	You should save for big purchases, and learn how to defer pleasure.
I can worship God anywhere. In the forest, at work, in the street, at a concert.	I find meaning in God's sanctuary. There are so many memories with this place.
I can find spiritual insight anywhere. Even with other major world religions. I can do Yoga, read the wisdom of Confucius, even attend different churches.	You pick a denomination and stick with it. If you are Christian, you reject other religious views.
I gain my spiritual strength from a small group of friends. We are very "tight" with each other and would do anything for each other.	My church provides me a great social network, and I so appreciate the church's prayers for me and my family in our time of need.

This table lists generalizations, but they reflect some truths about the ways in which people think. Just ponder how difficult it would be for a young adult to accept any religious authority from anyone. They witnessed the fall of several TV evangelists in their lives. They know of religious leaders in community churches who have had ethical problems. They know of fallen CEOs, bankers, politicians, and even a President of the United States who left office under disgrace.

If we lump all of the younger cohort groups together (basically those younger than Baby Boomers), they represent 65 percent of the U.S. population.[22] Yet this large segment is largely missing in our worship attendance today.

As I continued my conversation with my seatmate, I discovered some real differences in his mind-set from mine. He was talking about all the advanced computer work he had done in college, and I was thinking of my computer science class. I had to go to the library where there was a huge mainframe computer and six stations for students. I had to use a teletype and paper tape. And at the end of the semester I got it to balance my checkbook. This young man could never remember a time when he didn't have access to a computer. He grew up knowing when to push "enter" and how to click and point. He could make his computer dance.

We talked about movies. I can't remember his favorite movie…it had no meaning to me. I do remember he made fun of Star Wars and how fake it was. I didn't share with him that I waited in line for two hours in San Francisco to watch it when it first came out in a theater that had surround sound. I didn't want the ridicule.

When we talked politics, he didn't know that there had been an assassination attempt on Ronald Reagan. Reagan had been President most of his life, but he had no idea about his politics. He only had heard of the Vietnam War in his history class.

He had never heard the phrase "Where's the beef?" He never knew a time when the Titanic's location was unknown. And for him Michael Jackson had always been a *former* rock star.

The whole time we were talking he was multitasking. He was connecting his iPod to his computer to upload new music. He had several windows open on his computer at the same time, searching for his recent downloads and for e-mail that he saved on his computer before the flight. He ordered a drink and never paused our conversation.

It reminded me of my son. When he was in high school, I went downstairs to ask him to move his car. He was listening to music, playing a video game, and watching TV simultaneously. I felt ignored. When I asked him to repeat what I had just requested, he did so without missing a beat.

Young adults today can multitask. Yet in many of our churches we only offer a single channel of communication. We talk at them. And worse yet, it is only a one-way conversation. That may be why emergent congregations and churches that offer multimedia are growing in the context we have today.

The final thing I learned from this young man was that he had no desire to "join" anything. Instead, his affiliation with groups was very voluntary, provided they were doing something of value. He was not going to be a part of the machinery of organizing just for the point of organizing. It had to be of value.

Michael Foss, a Lutheran pastor, wrote an excellent book entitled *Power Surge*,[23] which addresses some of our generational disconnects. He states that the church is *not* a membership organization, but a group that is committed to "discipleship." His congregation today engages thousands of people across generational lines.

Most membership organizations act alike. When you become a member, you can expect to pay dues, sign on a line. When you do that, you can expect care, access, privilege, control, and service from the staff.

For example, if you join a health club, you will sign the membership forms. When you come the next week, you will have a locker, towel, a trainer named Vic, and at the end of your workout a good soak in the hot tub, with people calling you by name and smiling.

In some ways this is what congregations have become. You "join" the church and then you get your place to sit on Sundays (usually the same seat), you can expect the pastor to call on you if you go to the hospital (even if you didn't tell the pastor you were having surgery), and you expect to have the "privilege" of voting at congregational meetings, taking communion, and volunteering for whatever you feel like doing.

The word *membership* does not appear in scripture. It really didn't apply to church life until the eighteenth century and actually became more formal in the early nineteenth century. It is a way of distinguishing those who "belong" to this church from those who "don't belong" to it. When you think about it, it is a form of exclusion that is antithetical to the Gospel.

When my young seatmate thinks about the church, he is thinking about it as a private organization, not a place where he can grow closer to God in his faith journey. He also sees it as a place of exclusion, especially in regard to his friends who have different lifestyles. He does not see why churches argue about the so-called "gay issue" at all. He has no use for groups that keep others out. In fact most of the postmodern world does not.

That explains why organizations such as the Elks, Kiwanis, and scouting groups, among others, are struggling with declining numbers today. The notion of exclusion is not a part of the postmodern world mind-set.

However, this young man does seek to serve others. He has a global view and a desire to be a part of something that is making a difference. Remember, he gave his time as a student to go to Central America and rebuild after a storm.

Today, 60 percent of college students study abroad.[24] Most graduates today have a good idea of what it is like to live in another country. It used to be that churches were the window to a global perspective through missionary efforts. But today, when a missionary visits a church, he or she will likely meet someone who has been to his or her country before through a school or other organization.

Because of this global perspective, young people are interested in how God is working in the world, not just our backyard, or not just within our small church. They want to see the difference the church makes globally, and they would be willing to be a part of that.

Young adults will give time to build a house for Habitat. They will give time to clean up a neighborhood or help a family in distress. But they will *not* attend a committee meeting to discuss the table centerpieces for the next church potluck, they do not want to nominate officers for the church, and refuse to haggle over $100 in the church budget.

I was a visiting preacher at a church was and was invited to join the congregation at the church dinner afterward. I agreed to this without knowing that they were having their congregational meeting in between. The congregation had an animated, lengthy conversation about the term "restricted funds" and whether there should be a budgeted amount for them on the income side. They spent forty-five minutes in this painful discussion and finally established a smaller committee to make a recommendation to them at their next meeting. The line item amount was $250. The congregation spent an enormous amount of volunteer time, which will turn into a committee, for just a $250 figure on a budget they will vote on. I was so glad none of my seatmates were with me at that church.

Choices

Unspoken by all three of these seatmates was that all of them had more choices today than people their same age did just fifteen years ago. If there is anything that can be said of this time in the United States, it is that we are a consumer society. Consider the following:[25]

- Americans constitute 5 percent of the world's population but consume 24 percent of the world's energy.
- On average, one American consumes as much energy as
    - ~ 2 Japanese
    - ~ 6 Mexicans
    - ~ 13 Chinese
    - ~ 31 Indians
    - ~ 128 Bangladeshis
    - ~ 307 Tanzanians
    - ~ 370 Ethiopians
- Americans eat 815 billion calories of food each day—that's roughly 200 billion more than needed.
- Americans throw out 200,000 tons of edible food daily.
- The average American generates 52 tons of garbage by age 75.
- The average individual's daily consumption of water is 159 gallons, while more than half the world's population lives on 25 gallons.
- Fifty percent of the wetlands, 90 percent of the Northwestern old-growth forests, and 99 percent of the tall-grass prairie have been destroyed in the last 200 years.
- Eighty percent of the corn grown and 95 percent of the oats are fed to livestock.
- Fifty-six percent of available farmland is used for beef production.
- Every day an estimated nine square miles of rural land are lost to development.
- The United States has more shopping malls than high schools.

Many use the term *postmodern* to describe our times, which involve living in a more complex world of numerous choices.

When the church came into dominance in Europe in the Middle Ages, it was the only power. It was the political seat of a community; it was the court; it provided education; and the "parish" denoted a community for which the church provided services, with everyone in the parish attending that church. There were few choices. If a storm hit that city, people would run to the church and consult the priest as to why God was angry at them.

In the "modern" world that soon followed, science also became a force. Faith and reason began to work sometimes in harmony, other times in dissonance. The world of science first emerged as a discipline within theological studies, but soon became a force within itself. Then, through the philosophy of John Locke, faith and reason began to diverge. It is fascinating that today the U.S. Constitution is still greatly influenced by the concepts of Locke and focused on government being administered by reason.

In the modern world, a storm could hit a city, and people would consult the priest. They could also ask science about the natural phenomena's that lead to the storm and be satisfied.

Today, however, our postmodern world has moved from the two channels of faith and reason to more than 500 channels of choice. Faith and reason alone do not provide enough answers for people today, and they turn to hundreds of choices for their main source of understanding.

A trend that I noticed while serving my last congregation was that of "consumer worship." There was a growing number of people whom I would see in worship periodically, who would disappear for months at a time and then return out of the blue. I visited personally with a number of them and discovered for myself what was happening.

People began to look at congregations as they did any other consumer organization. Whoever was offering what they needed for that moment was where they would attend. One woman stated that her husband was very conservative in his beliefs, and that if he was going to worship with her that day, they would go to one of a number of different Southern Baptist congregations in our area. If he was staying home to watch football, she would either attend our church, or one of a number of other ecumenically minded congregations in the area. If she had her stepchildren, they would attend the megachurch in our community because the kids liked the music.

She is a product of postmodernism, discovering the choices she can make by bouncing from church to church. Sometimes her family does not feel any need to be a part of a church and they attend nowhere in particular. Since she has erratic patterns, there is no expectation from any congregation.

Today, when a storm hits a city, people no longer ask the priest or the scientist for an explanation. Now they consult the Internet and learn from all kinds of perspectives, such as newscasters on BBC, or

Native American shamans, or the neighborhood Sikh Holy man. The choices for information are just about infinite.

This leads to a final concept known as "postdenominationalism". The term was first coined by Bill Easum and was met with a lot of rejection by those of us who are denominational leaders.

I have to admit that when I first began to understand the term, I was angry. How could anyone claim my denomination could not be relevant to the postmodern world! After all, denominations have checks and balances in place to ensure quality for our clergy and congregations. Yet as I study the data, it is becoming clear that our connectedness to each other has become less valued, even within churches in our denominations.

Nothing points this out more clearly than how local congregations spend their money. Few historians chart spending patterns of congregations. However, I have heard over the years lots of anecdotal evidence of mission giving patterns. An elderly member of a congregation in Tennessee once told me of a time in which his church raised enough money in one day to build an education wing on their facility. He stated that the congregation could only do so by raising equal dollars for mission. The motto of their financial campaign was "$1 for missions, and $1 for us." There are few if any congregations within our denomination that raise any mission dollars while fundraising for a building campaign because that would be seen as a deterrent to the building campaign.

Another colleague of mine saw a historical certificate from her congregation from the 1930s that recognized the church's giving 30 percent of their income toward the greater mission of the "brotherhood."

When I looked at giving patterns for our denomination (the Disciples of Christ) in 1995, it appeared our average congregation voluntarily contributed 6 percent of its general fund income toward "Disciple causes." Today that number is closer to 3 percent on average.

Part of the reason for this is the vast number of choices congregations have in supporting the mission of other parachurch and nonprofit organizations that provide for basic human needs. (The high cost of sustaining congregations is another reason that will be discussed in the next chapter). The reality is that more and more congregations are focusing spending on themselves.

Local congregations look outside their walls with some fear about what the world is becoming. Now that church people are a minority of the population (only 49 percent)[26] we are becoming more like those pioneers who built forts to keep out the local native populations. That is not an attractive metaphor for the church, and is in no way supported theologically or biblically.

Talking to those not involved in a church is a powerful experience, and I would encourage you to have conversations with people in your community. It is far more insightful than any book you can read. Unfortunately, many of us in church have become what William Willimon would call "Resident Aliens." That is, we are foreigners in our own context who have built fences around our churches to protect us from the wilderness of the unchurched.[27]

Local congregations look outside their walls with some fear about what the world is becoming. Now that church people are a minority of the population (only 49%)[28] we are becoming more like those pioneers who built forts to keep out the local native populations. That is not an attractive metaphor for the church, and is in no way supported theologically or biblically.

The history of the church over the past 2,000 years has been a story of people coming to grips with their culture, and having the Gospel make sense to their context. From the early Roman period, to the Middle Ages and the Reformation, to the start of the American religious experience, people like us have found ways to allow others to see the value of what the church can offer in order that ordinary people might live extraordinary lives.

Our culture today is at a tipping point. Christianity in our North American culture will either take root in a new way, or it will become like churches in Europe, which are largely museums honoring the past. It is all a matter of people wanting to answer the questions that are being asked today, or continue with the rituals and traditions that answer the questions no one is asking.

I shared the stories of just three of many seatmates I have had the joy of meeting while traveling. These encounters have numerous lessons for the church, and I would encourage you to have similar conversations with your fellow travelers. Without casting judgement, what are people telling us? What are the openings we might have to lead them to the living Christ? How can we adapt our churches to engage the very people who would benefit the most from a relationship with Christ and his church?

Questions for Discussion

1. What were the three profiles of seatmates discussed in this chapter?

2. Can you name a profile of someone you know who is not a part of a faith community, and some of the reasons that person does not participate?
3. What are some of the factors leading to the decline in church participation today?
4. There were many topics in this chapter. Which issue do you think has the most impact on our congregation today?
    a. Shifting cultural values
    b. Globalization of the community
    c. Mobility rates of families
    d. Lack of generational continuity
    e. Lower birth rates
    f. Lack of adapting to younger generational needs
    g. Disconnect with the unchurched
5. Which of the topics on this list have the least impact on our congregation?

2

Exegete Your Community

When pastors attend seminary much time is spent in "exegesis," which is the critical explanation or interpretation of a text or portion of the Bible. Pastors are taught to use their understanding of biblical languages, earlier renderings of the text, cross references with other ancient documents, and more in order to understand the passage from many different angles. Pastors are not taught how to apply the same critical skills toward understanding their communities. That is the work leaders do together.

The first lens an image passes through is the objective lens. It is large and magnifies the image of our future, but by itself it is distorted. Because this lens is so large, a small distance must separate the two objective lenses. In order to get the image back to the eyes of the observer, they must pass through two prisms.

This first prism is our reflection of our community. The issues of postmodernity hit communities at different times. Perhaps your

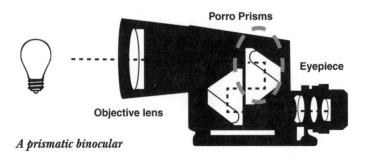

A prismatic binocular

community is not dealing with mobility issues. Perhaps your community is isolated from the globalization that impacts most places. Every community is unique, and the human dynamics that propel them are unique.

A congregation I once served liked to be on the "cutting edge." What we did there years ago seems pretty tame today, but being a new church meant we could try many new things. We were one of the first churches in our area that projected the words of *hymns* on the wall during worship. We had a carousel projector, and a company that could produce slides. When we first set it up, the perfect platform was the 6-foot stepladder out of the closet. We took the ladder out, flopped down the paint stand, and plugged in the projector to flash the images on the wall. We were proud of our innovative abilities, and the worshiping community loved the images.

A couple of years later, we performed a wedding for a young man who was in the military and his bride. She came from another community, and we were doing all we could to make her wedding day perfect. When the wedding coordinator asked her, "Can we do anything else before the big day?" she said "Yes, do you think we could lose the ladder?"

Our congregation had grown so used to the ladder that we failed to even notice it anymore. It sat there week after week holding the projector. It was part of our environment. But when the bride-to-be mentioned it looked a "little tacky" for her wedding day, we knew we had to change.

When you live in a community, you often fail to recognize the stepladder in the corner. The reason is because the changes that occur in communities are slow and subtle. It is not unusual to meet with congregational leaders and discover that they still believe their community is much like it was twenty years ago, when the reality has changed dramatically.

That is why we need to look at our community more closely and perhaps with new eyes.

In this chapter we look at community dynamics and how they impact congregations. At the end we outline a process by which you can look at your community through new eyes.

The Power of Context

In 2001, the Winchester Heights Christian church in Memphis, Tennessee, discovered they had a broken water heater. They only had eleven members and were in debt to their pastor by at least $5,000 in back salary. The congregation made a decision to close and give the assets to a new church.

This was a congregation started in the 1950s, in a suburban, segregated Anglo community. The congregation thrived during that time, averaging about 160 in worship. In the 1980s Fed Ex moved their international headquarters to the Winchester Heights area, and the community blossomed. The company increased the racial diversity of the community and brought executives from all over the country to it. By the 1990s Fed Ex had grown out of its facilities and relocated the company further south. Lots of housing went on the market at one time, and the largest racial group among buyers was first-time African American homeowners.

The Winchester Heights congregation grew smaller. It did nothing to adapt to its changing context. It continued to worship in styles that meant nothing to the rapidly growing African American population. Participants' average age grew older while the community was becoming much younger. They used a pipe organ, sang 200-year-old music, read litanies, and had little in common with the preaching style of the African American church. They did what they knew best as well as they could, but there were few in this new context who could relate to it, and so they completed their ministry.

A new congregation named New Direction Christian Church started in the same building one month later under the dynamic leadership of Dr. Stacey Spencer. Dr. Spencer had been a leader in the community and worked at a large African American congregation in central Memphis named Mississippi Boulevard Christian church. The first Sunday, Dr. Spencer counted more than 400 in worship (in a sanctuary that seated only 200). The second Sunday more than 700, and in just seven years the congregation now includes more tha 6,000 worshipers on a Sunday.

Context was everything in this case. New Direction's target group was young, African American men who had a need for strong identity and a desire to become leaders in a community that was increasingly changing. This vital congregation has made a huge difference in its community; today it provides leadership in the Memphis metropolitan area on many fronts.[1] The church has also sponsored two new congregations, which are also contextually relevant.

Context is everything. You can have a great congregation, with a pastor who preaches outstanding sermons, an excellent music program, an excellent education program, but if it is located in the wrong place the congregation will still suffer.

There is a definite link between churches that are contextually relevant and their ability to succeed. Simply put, the congregation must be answering the questions the community is asking.

Discovering Your Community

Psychological Boundaries

Not long ago a congregation in a major city was perplexed by its inability to attract people from a neighboring affluent area. The affluent area was just to the northeast of their community, and had easy access to their church. The congregation was located in an area with a lower household income, and the church was suffering financially. "All we need is a couple of wealthy individuals in our church and we would be set!" was the thinking.

While there is a lot wrong with this kind of thinking from a theological and ethical standpoint, there are also some major issues from a sociological standpoint. The congregation was hoping that the people in the affluent area would cross significant psychological barriers and enter their area, which was not likely to happen without denominational loyalty (a quality that rarely exists today).

Every community has boundaries. They are usually called the "city limits." These boundaries, however, become more and more meaningless as time goes on. Most metropolitan communities today have no buffer zone between communities. Without a sign you cannot tell where one community begins and another ends.

In every city, different people groups live in distinct parts of the community. This is true even in small towns. That is why when we define communities, we talk about psychological boundaries. These boundaries define communities without the use of signs or fences, and they are very real.

The phrase "the other side of the tracks" is a way of speaking of psychological boundaries in our culture. The people who lived on one side of the railroad tracks were very different from those who lived on the other side. Tracks are still a boundary, but so are freeways, geographical features such as hills and mountains, lakes and streams. Even irrigation ditches can serve as boundaries.

A psychological boundary is defined by physical features such as tracks, freeways, or geology, which create a subconsciously defined area that creates an area of comfort for its inhabitants.

The congregation above was hoping that people would cross the psychological boundaries of the river and the freeway to enter into their area. While people will freely cross these borders for work, and even some for shopping, they tend to organize the rest of their lives largely within these boundaries. Banks discovered this concept years ago when they began creating small branch offices to make banking accessible. Grocery stores know that people will not travel great distances for their food. That is why most of their marketing strategies include discovering the psychological boundaries of areas and how they can best relate to their areas.

The congregation was also hoping that the affluent people would move into an area with a significantly different people group. We will discuss people groups later.

Things That Define Psychological Boundaries
Freeways or Highways

In the 1940s, there was a strong congregation on the east side of Spokane, Washington, named Garfield Avenue Christian Church. This congregation boasted a worship attendance of 400, and had a large Sunday school. Each week the church building was stretched to capacity with multiple services, children, and valuable ministries to their growing community.

The church was located between the main residential area and the primary shopping district. In those days of one-car families it was the perfect location. People would have to pass the church to go to work, shop for goods, or even take a vacation. It was just a few blocks from the main east-west highway in and out of the city. It was perfect until the new freeway was completed in the early 1960s.

When completed, the freeway bisected the residential area and turned Garfield Avenue into a dead-end street. The church lost the visibility of an important artery.

Soon the businesses that were once neighborhood retail stores became light industrial space. The neighborhood retail core worked its way toward the artery that had access to the freeway. After years of decline and a host of short-term pastorates, the church closed in the late 1980s.

Part of the issue was that the congregation failed to recognize the impact of its psychological boundaries, which had changed forever. They acted as if the freeway weren't there, or didn't matter, and did their best to keep the church functioning with lower numbers. Had the church recognized this changing dynamic and relocated north of the freeway, where they had their most affinity, they would likely still be an active faith community today.

Following World War II, when President Eisenhower developed the freeway system, new suburbs spread out across the United States and outlying areas became much closer. Suburbs began to flourish, and people left the cities for larger lots and places to park their cars. Few people could have predicted the impact that the U.S. freeway system would have on our communities. This was especially true for the pre-1940s congregations.

Being too close to a freeway can have an impact on a congregation's ability to grow. This is the impact of the invisible barrier of congestion. People will avoid areas that are known for congestion.

For example, Creighton Christian Church in Phoenix is located right on a freeway access and is struggling to revitalize its ministry. Numerous dynamics relate to this, but the fact that the church is located too close to a freeway also plays into the equation.

The congregation is located within a block of the freeway access, which has a heavy volume of traffic with lengthy traffic lights. The congestion associated with these high traffic areas can become a barrier to church participation. Not having right-of-entry from the main street in both directions can be a real obstacle to congregational growth, especially if you have to go around the block and wait through long traffic lights.

Congestion, even away from a freeway, creates an avoidance zone for potential participants. While a congregation may gain great visibility from the site, local residents (your best prospects) will avoid the area at all costs.

By contrast, easy access to a freeway (without congestion) can play heavily in a church's ability to spread its net. "Drive time" is a term used to describe an irregular circle stretched around a congregation. It is irregular because of physical boundaries, traffic choke points, and the speed limits of the streets. Malls locate near freeways, and often at places where freeways intersect with each other. This is because these highways make it possible for many more customers to get to their stores within a small time frame.

Middletown Christian Church is adjacent to a largely upper middle-class residential area that is a commuter community to nearby Louisville. It is located near one of the largest churches in Kentucky, and the congregation today is growing dramatically under the leadership of Pastor David Emory. Its location is adjacent to an area in which housing is 92 percent owner occupied. This congregation is

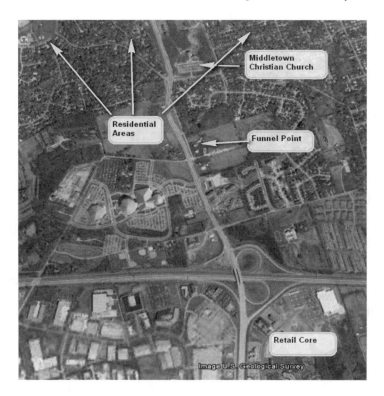

Middletown
Christian Church

Residential
Areas

Funnel Point

Retail Core

Image U.S. Geological Survey

growing because of excellent leadership and a hot target area. Its accessibility to the freeway does not hurt.

As you can see, the natural flow of traffic takes a large growing population past the church building every time people go to work or shopping. It is visible and takes advantage of its unique mission that contrasts that of the neighboring megachurch. People who may have been drawn initially to the megachurch can see the value of a good-sized congregation just across the street that doesn't require traffic control. When they get there, they can engage in a quality ministry program.

Freeways are a two-edged sword, and they can impact a church's ability to relate to its community.

Topography

Topographical barriers are another consideration. Housing cannot be built on a river or lake, and it is more costly to build on the side of a steep hill. The geology of an area can be a factor too. If the ground is solid rock, or sinking swamp, there will be no future development of that area until the density and value of housing make it financially feasible. People tend to think of these features as defining their community, and refer to other places as "the other side of the river." Even though the feature may be small, it impacts the way we think about our community.

Business and Industrial Boundaries

Industrial and business districts create boundaries. Dense retail business districts have little housing in them. Communities that develop south of a mall, for example, have different characteristics from those who are on the north side. This has a lot to do with traffic patterns. People will avoid congested areas in everyday life, thus creating a boundary. Even though the people on the north side shop in the same mall, it is a clear boundary.

Numerous new congregations have failed at establishing themselves in light-industrial areas. These are not the kinds of districts that people pass through unless they work there. We cannot list all of the potential psychological boundaries, but obviously manufacturing areas, refineries, airports, heavy industrial areas, light industrial areas, and more all play into this concept.

Invisible Congregations

Obviously, a congregation that is located in the middle of a residential area on a street with very little traffic will have difficulty reaching sustainability. For a period of time in the 1950s, many congregations were located in these communities in areas we characterize as being "three blocks from success." Believe it or not, a congregation can be located on a very busy street and still be invisible as well.

In the 1970s and '80s it became stylish to blend church buildings in with the surrounding community so much that you can hardly find them, even when you are looking. The churches are built like every other structure on the street, and often have such overgrown landscaping you cannot see the church. Coupled with not having a sign, or a sign that was hand-painted on plywood in someone's garage, these congregations do not take advantage of the passive evangelism their buildings might bring.

I was having trouble locating a church once even with a GPS guiding me. It kept telling me I was driving by the church, but I failed to see it. I did something I rarely do–I asked for directions at a next-door convenience store. The people working there knew nothing about the church. When I found it (right next door), it was located across the street from the regional Super Wal-Mart, behind a huge barrier of shrubs and trees. I felt as if I were in a James Bond movie where the bad guy disguised his hideout. Churches can make capital improvements that would lead to better visibility. Merely changing the color of the building can be a vast improvement. A back-lit sign with movable type can also improve the congregation's visibility, particularly if that sign posts program opportunities for neighboring participants. Before investing in such signs, however, check with the local officials about laws governing signs.

While some communities require certain numbers of trees and other items that hide churches, care can be given in planning to capitalize on visibility while meeting the codes. It just takes some intentionality in the planning process.

People Groups

The congregation at the start of this chapter wanted to draw people from an affluent group into their community across a number of psychological boundaries. The other consideration they did not take into account was that they were asking them to move into another people group.

Marketers have spent a lot of time researching people groups. They know *a lot* about the common behaviors of different groups of people. Once they know a few key facts about an individual, they can almost predict what medium that person will get their news from, how comfortable the person will be with Internet shopping, what kind of car the person will likely purchase, or even what magazine the person would select from a pile.

Churches have started to understand the need for giving attention to people groups. When Saddleback Community Church began, they were very intentional about developing a profile of the type of people they were seeking to attract with their ministry.

"Saddleback Sam" is a well-educated young professional. He is self-satisfied and comfortable with his life. He likes his job and where he lives. He is affluent, recreation conscious, and prefers the casual and informal over the formal. He is interested in health and fitness, and he thinks he is enjoying life more than he did five years ago, but he is overextended in time and money and is stressed out. He has some religious background from childhood, but he hasn't been to church for fifteen or twenty years, and he is skeptical of "organized religion." He doesn't want to be recognized when he comes to church.

While some may have reservations about being this specific about a target for ministry, you cannot discount the success of Saddleback in focusing a ministry that meets a target. It does not exclude people from other people groups from attending. It just assures that people from the Saddleback Sam group have their needs met.

In each people group are several subgroups that marketers have begun to isolate and analyze. One such paradigm is MOSAIC.[2] This paradigm is a listing of twelve main groupings of people that breaks down to sixty subtypes. This kind of information can be very powerful for a congregation that is attempting to meet the concerns of a certain group of people in their community.

MOSAIC was developed as a market research tool for financial institutions, and has now spread to many other business sectors. You can find examples of MOSAIC graphics on the Internet.

Let us consider a group known as "Moderate Conventionalists." The Mosaic analysis would allow you to see that this group likes to shop at Best Buy and will stock up on fat-free foods. Economic health is important to them, so they save money. They are largely in their forties to sixties in age, and they work in management positions. You can see what they like to watch on TV, the kinds of cars they enjoy driving, the values of their homes, and the Web sites they visit. It even can give you typical names of the people who live in the subset.

This information is powerful for understanding the kinds of programs and ministries a church would need to do for this subgroup, such as a faith-based financial planning program. It also would demonstrate the times for ministry, the location, the kind of space in which they would feel comfortable, the amount of media they would be comfortable with etc.

Another factor for consideration in working with people groups is their upward movement. People will likely gravitate upward in a socioeconomic group, striving to improve their situation. They will attend a congregation in a socioeconomic group that is just above their current situation. They will rarely attend a church with a group that is one or two steps below their perceived place on the socioeconomic spectrum.

A community in Texas demonstrates this as well. This suburb of a city is boxed-in by freeways. However, a rapidly changing area that is becoming more affluent is included in that area. Wealthy Texans, wanting to shorten their commutes, have replaced their old homes with large "McMansions." Amenities include a country club and private, exclusive schools, among other things. This has impacted a local congregation that had a mission focus that was relevant fifty years ago.

However, some communities have been segregated intentionally. "Redlining" is an unlawful and discriminatory practice involving lenders who refuse to lend money or extend credit to borrowers in certain "struggling" areas of town. It is against the law to discriminate against borrowers based on race or income level, among other factors. Redlining became known as such because lenders would draw a red line around a neighborhood on a map, often targeting areas with a high concentration of minorities, and then refusing to lend in those areas because they considered the risk too high. Even though it is now against the law, some lenders today are still accused of redlining.[3]

This area that was once homogenous (first-time suburban home-owners) is changing, and the church is right in the middle of it. The congregation today draws people from the middle-class area. However, that area has continuously shrunk, and the dynamics of the area are changing. In this case, the psychological boundaries for this area are outside of the physical location of the church building. People in the middle class area may go to the affluent mall on occasion as a treat, or head to the lower-middle class grocery store for a sale, but their comfort zone is clearly different.

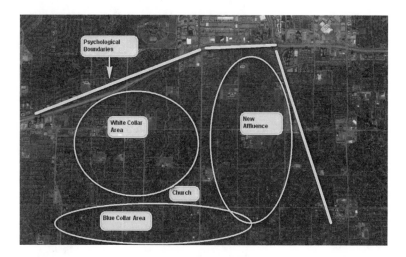

Meanwhile, the growing affluent group will not go to the Dollar Store (except in a disguise). Those who live in the "blue collar" area will only occasionally treat themselves to services or stores in the affluent area. The church, which at one time drew people from the entire area, is in a ministry quandary. Do they attempt to shift their ministry toward meeting the needs of those in the growing affluent people group, or shift toward the needs of the declining blue-collar group? That kind of decision will require deep discernment of the scriptures, as well as insight into the changing community dynamics.

For some congregations the church building location may have nothing to do with the people group that meets in the building. We have run across this phenomena several times in the past few years as demonstrated in the map below.

This kind of dynamic cannot sustain a congregation. When the target group of the congregation has little in common with the people who live within the psychological boundaries of an area, ministry becomes very difficult.

In another Texan congregation, members were asked about the people who lived in their community: they knew nothing about them. When asked, "What would this community miss if this church was no longer present?" the room was silent. Finally someone said, "They

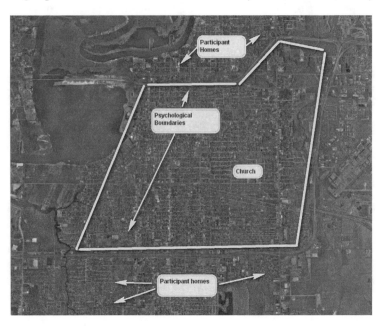

wouldn't miss a thing, they don't even know we are here today." This sad indictment led the congregation to close several months later.

Chapter 4 will cover the many strategies for congregations in this configuration.

Not long ago we were working with a congregation in Lake Charles, Louisiana. This fine congregation had leaders who were highly educated professionals trying to do church in a community that had changed its racial and educational profile considerably in the past twenty years. They were teachers, social workers, and even accountants. None of them lived in the area where the church was located.

By contrast, the community in which the church was located was composed mostly of blue collar and service workers, few of whom owned their own homes. The average education level of the area ranged from "some college" to "some high school." They were largely the working poor.

Needless to say, these leaders had a huge disconnect with the people groups in their area of ministry, and little ability to excel in ministry for their most likely participants. This leads us to conclude that a church must have some connection with its immediate community.

Community Life-cycle

For years bankers have understood that communities have life-cycles. At one time this knowledge led to the dynamic of "red-lining" areas with a high population of racial ethnic residents. However, some rules and cooler heads have led to great models of revitalizing communities today by investing in places that seemed on their way out.

Congregations must understand where their community is in its life-cycle today. The mission objectives for a congregation fifty years ago, or perhaps even ten years ago, cannot be the same today since their community has likely changed significantly.

There has been some extensive research on community life-cycle. In 2000, John T. Metzger wrote a paper entitled "Planned Abandonment: The Neighborhood Life-cycle Theory and National Urban Policy."[4] Metzger drew analysis from national studies over the past seventy years about community life-cycles. It is difficult to read that data without acknowledging the truth he demonstrates that communities go through the same growth and decline. (*Please see Appendix A for a chart about these studies*)

If a congregation can identify the point at which a community is in its life-cycle, it can create ministries that are contextually relevant. If not, the congregation will continue to offer ministry that only meets the community dynamics of another time.

The Suburban Context

Northside Christian Church began in the 1950s when the Gateway Area organized the development of the church in what were then the rapidly growing suburbs of St. Louis. Its original mission was to serve the Disciples moving from the city into this suburban area. The congregation was formed in 1954 (about ten years after the area developed significantly). At today's site, the church built its first unit in 1958, and it was almost filled immediately. In 1970 the congregation built its sanctuary and additional classrooms.

A spot check of congregation data submitted to the Yearbook (the annual report for Disciples congregations) indicates that the congregation hit a peak in the 1960s and began its decline in the 1970s. Based on accepted averages, we can estimate that the congregation's average worship attendance (AWA) in the '60s was around 200. In 1975 we can estimate the AWA at 160, and in 1985 it had dropped to 105 (as reported).

According to city planners, the mid-1970s was a time of large cultural shifts in this part of St. Louis. By 1973 the area had completed thirteen subsidized housing units and the racial make-up of the area began to change. According to the Castle Point neighborhood plan, African American families in the area were harassed, and many Anglos left the area abruptly.

The area changed significantly. As the original residents of the houses around the church left, a growing number of upwardly mobile African Americans moved into the area. The racial mix reached a tipping point in the early 1990s, as the phenomenon of "white flight" hit Northside hard.

The congregation has continued to decline for more than twenty years, mostly because it cannot replace those leaving the church with a ministry program that is focused on what is now a very small segment of the population of the community. Today this church, which once had 200 people worshiping on Sunday morning, averages just 36 people.

This congregation's setting demonstrates several dynamics that take place in the life-cycle of a suburban community. Suburban communities usually develop within a period of ten to fifteen years.

That includes the first subdivision, the development of infrastructure, and the development of a retail core to saturation of land. Of course, these time frames vary. Following this development, the community may increase its density if it continues to grow, or the new development may spread to the next parcels in outward spirals from the city.

When a community first develops, it is attractive because it is new and usually less costly than living in the population center. It doesn't have adjacent medical services, and little retail outside of a grocery store. It provides a fairly rural feeling, with large properties without development. Those who live there must be willing to drive *a lot*. The group attracted to this kind of community can be called "pioneers." They are willing to try something new, live in a land of "promise" and have some faith that the rest of the services will follow them soon. Homeownership among this group is over 95 percent. They see their property as an investment. Pioneers have no trouble attending a new church meeting in a school building.

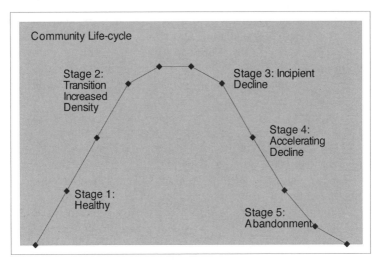

As the community develops and population grows, a market-driven retail core starts to emerge, and some medical services become available to the community. Population density increases, and some rental units emerge. Homeownership drops to about 88 percent. Some pioneers have already had to relocate, and given that there are so many new houses on the market, they choose to rent out their property. The people that move into this kind of housing are "settlers". They choose to live there not just because of the lower cost associated with the area but also because it is a great place to raise a family. It has new schools, new stores, and very low crime. The settlers are more stable and they hope to retire in their home (even though that is not likely). They will attend a church in a school briefly, but the first church to build will likely attract them if it has adequate programs for their family.

As property becomes more scarce and saturated, the density will increase even more. The community, which was once dependent on jobs in adjacent communities, now has an economy of its own, with a growing number of workers in the community, usually in service jobs. A community at this point may take a big leap if a large company chooses to locate its headquarters there. This increases the affluence of the area.

If the community takes this turn, it will redevelop its housing, accommodating the new households moving to the area. A hospital will likely soon follow, and a new mall will be opened.

If the community does not attract a major business, but is located at the junction of two major freeways or even a major state road and a freeway, a large new mall may be built. This increases employment, but homeownership rates will drop to 60 percent. Commerce will be good, but the trade will come from people outside the area. The non-commuting population will be serving people from other communities.

The people who live in these areas are a mixture of settlers and tenants. That is, a significant part of the population will view their participation in this community as temporary, and will not likely stay over the long term. Two kinds of churches exist in this context: those who quickly assimilate people into full participation, and settler congregations that provide steady programs for families.

When the community begins to reach forty to fifty years of age it has taken one of two paths, depending on the development surrounding the community. If the surrounding areas have continued to increase population density, the housing in this area is still of high value, and new homeowners will continue to improve and update the housing. They will retain a high percentage of homeownership (more than 60 percent), and the housing costs will appreciate greatly. The retail core will redevelop and improve to compete with new retail outside of the area. These people will want to attend a full-service congregation with settler attitudes. While they may be still highly mobile, they will seek stability.

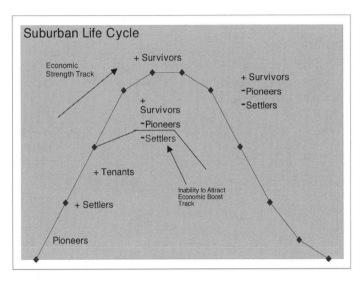

If the adjacent area does not continue to grow, and new suburbs are built in outlying areas, the community will begin to stagnate. The housing style will no longer attract the up-and-coming parts of the population. Those attracted to this community now are "survivors." They have enough money to move into a house, but not enough to continually improve or maintain it. Homeownership drops to 50 percent or lower. The retail core begins to show more vacancies, crime increases, and schools begin to deteriorate because of the erosion of the tax base. At this point there are settlers, tenants, and "survivors" in the community.

When the percentage of survivors hits a tipping point, the community will begin to accelerate its decline. The need for social services increases. As the settlers leave the community, new opportunities for housing open up for first-generation immigrants, who tend to informally move as groups to specific areas. They maintain homeownership and change the racial ethnic composition of the community. At this point the community is looking for fast assimilation, perhaps racial ethnic congregations, and congregations devoted to local mission.

It should be noted that in the St. Louis example, in the area around Northside Christian, five Presbyterian congregations merged into one. The Catholic Church closed its parish, and only one Methodist Church remained in the community. Most of the congregations failed to adapt to their new reality.

This life-cycle model is a simplification of a very complex anthropological phenomenon. It is a model of community transition from suburban to metropolitan. Suburbs are largely dependent on the adjacent community's economic strength. As long as there are employment opportunities and a growing economic health of the general area, the suburban community will continue to reinvent itself and grow. Without that strength, it will likely decline.

Note which community your church is a part of, and the types of people who live there. What is their goal for living in that community? Are they there to settle and develop a family? Are they just there temporarily as they work for a better life elsewhere? Are they on fixed incomes, seeking hope for getting ahead? These are important things to keep in mind when developing ministry in a changing context.

In 2003 I began to work on a team that developed a new service at Church Extension (a national unit in the Disciples of Christ). This new service was called New Beginnings©, and was developed primarily for a growing number of congregations that were seriously struggling with sustainability issues for their ministry.

After a couple of years, I began to notice that each of the communities we were working in had some very similar dynamics. It was getting downright predictable! The communities in which these congregations were located were going through a life-cycle, and the church was not adapting to the changes that were occurring.

Our initial research revealed some significant findings. In the 1950s Disciples developed new congregations in 180 newly developed suburbs. Of those 180 congregations, only nine are sustainable by today's standards. The remaining congregations have either closed or are struggling with long periods of decline.

A lot of churches are in the same boat as the church in St. Louis. Suburbs develop, then the original owners leave, and a new community develops. Unlike communities in the past, where you would live in the same house from the time you married until you died, people are now highly mobile. Suburban communities develop over a short period of time. A group of people from different age groups move into the community and live a variety of lengths of time in their current home. The chart below demonstrates the length of time in which people of different ages have lived in their homes.[5]

Note that when a household leaves a community, its replacement is seldom identical. Different people groups come, bringing new attitudes and dreams. In the case of this St. Louis example, the community changed its racial composition. The congregation had

Characteristic		Percent who have lived in their present home...				Median years
		Less than 1 year	1 to 3 years	4 to 10 years	Over 10 years	
Total		18.7	24.7	26.7	30.0	4.7
Age						
15 to 24 years		32.6	26.8	25.9	14.7	2.3
25 to 34 years		31.0	40.4	22.9	5.6	1.9
35 to 44 years		17.1	28.6	36.4	17.9	4.3
45 to 54 years		11.6	19.0	29.1	40.3	8.0
55 to 64 years		8.2	14.4	22.6	54.8	12.2
65 years and older		5.7	10.1	18.7	65.5	18.7

fulfilled its mission among Anglo Disciples in that context. Today, they are considering new options for their future witness.

The fifty-year mark seems to be a factor. Over a fifty-year period you can guess that there are very few original owners of housing in a residential area. A new generation is now living in that area. This correlates with the life-cycle of congregations as well.

Congregations usually have a life-cycle of about eighty years unless the church reinvents itself, according to Lyle Schaller.[6] Some research I conducted on Disciples congregations that closed indicates that they averaged 67.3 years of age. I believe this is directly tied to the life-cycle of a community.

The Metropolitan Context

A classic example of metropolitan life-cycles comes from downtown Lincoln, Nebraska. Southview Christian Church was named "Tabernacle Christian Church" for the first fifty years of its existence. The church began in 1906 when the churches of Lincoln purchased property for a new church on what was then the south side of Lincoln.

In June of 1912, a large group of volunteers from Lincoln churches came together to build the Tabernacle church in just one day. They did not succeed because of the heat; however, within twelve hours these volunteers completed two-thirds of the church's first building, which served the new congregation for eight years.

In 1920 a decision was made to build a bigger building. After an extensive search for a site, a building was constructed at Southview's current location. The structure was built in 1923 and is the current space occupied by the office, fellowship hall, and Sunday school facilities (It was paid off in just one year!). The original structure looked like a castle, with three floors, though the third floor was removed some time later. It is estimated that in the 1930s the congregation had an average Sunday attendance of about 250. The Sunday school claimed 150 members.

By 1980 the congregation had declined to a comfortable 150 in worship. During that period Lincoln had grown. What was once the south side of Lincoln was now more like the central part of the city. Today, the church averages less than eighty in worship.

Like a tree, cities grow in rings. While they are not perfectly round, they still represent growth along arterials and freeways.

Every city has a core. This usually becomes a business core that squeezes out residential housing. As most cities began, their cores were small, and because of transportation, people tended to live in tight communities.

I have been to China several times, and I have noted that their communities are similar to American cities in the 1920s and '30s. Largely the reason for this is that very few people own a car. Within blocks of every location in their cities you have all the services you would need in any community. You can buy anything; the difference is that there are no parking lots, or large box stores. A car is a disadvantage in this setting, as there are no parking spaces. All local merchants work out of "garage-sized" shops selling batteries, suitcases, specific foods, and such. All within walking or biking distance. As oil becomes more expensive, it may be a trend Americans reconsider.

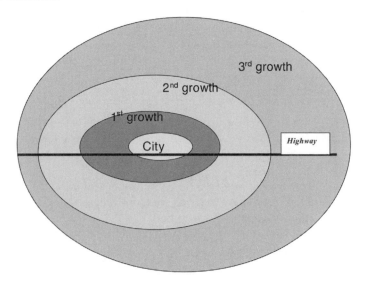

As the business core took over the downtown part of Lincoln, Nebraska, residential housing moved away from the core. In the early 1920s, people began to move around on trolleys, and then the automobile changed the development of our cities for good.

As the first ring opened up, people of means moved to that community. In many Midwest cities, we can still see the housing that those people bought. They were mostly large homes, well built, and with indoor plumbing. Ornamental casing work was done by hand saws, and these homes are a monument to craftsmanship not seen today. Others still lived in the core in apartments. These were the first suburbs and the residents of the first ring did their shopping in the city core. Housing was very mixed. There would be mansions next to small houses.

The second ring of most cities was developed in the late '30s and '40s, after the Depression subsided. Housing in this ring was more modest than the first ring. This housing was not as well built; sometimes occupants built them. Because of the distance to the city, people in these rings began to shop in small hardware and grocery stores near their homes. Residents would still go to the city for soft goods and professional services, such as medical and dental work. These houses often had detached garages for the family's one automobile.

The third ring of most cities developed after WWII. This ring of housing recognized the permanence of the automobile and the homes started having attached garages. They were larger than second ring homes, and had more landscaping in keeping with the commercial areas of the newly growing suburbs. They had small shopping centers with parking lots rather than parking on the street.

The city core and these three rings were defined by the city limits. Suburbs developed once the city grew to its outer edges. People outside of those limits did not receive bus service, city garbage pickup, or lighting.

Today the first rings are areas of major transition in most cities. They are typified by a low number of homeowners, often high crime, and an unhealthy retail core. The second ring has a slightly higher number of homeowners, but is typified by either long-term residents who are now in their seventies or low-income new residents. The third core is still relatively healthy in many cities, occupied by long-term residents who are aging.

Churches in the first ring have a difficult time. Sometimes the residential population is declining in the first ring. Homeownership was only 23 percent in the Nebraska example, and the apartment vacancy rate was 68 percent. The residents of this area are very transient, not looking to put roots down in the community. They are by and large the survivors discussed earlier, and congregations that are effective here usually have to depend on outside sources of income so they can provide ministry services that are relevant to this population.

Sometimes a city will allow an area to "go to seed" like this, so that they can expand the business district. The reality for congregations here is that their population is transient and the density is declining. There are not as many opportunities for growth, and economic survival for the congregation is difficult.

Second ring communities today have less transition because their residents are slightly more stable. Not all of these households own a car, and many are dependent on public transportation. Their homes are in constant need of repair because of their age, and the neighborhood starts to show it. The long-term residents in this part of the city are either dying or moving out. In many cities in the United States today, these houses are gentrifying. That is to say, cities are investing in turning housing in this ring around and attracting people who have more money back into the area.

One such city is Indianapolis. The city, in partnership with local builders and corporations, has redeveloped blocks of the city at a time. Upgrading old housing with new interiors, updating windows and major overhauls, the city has been able to attract young families to live in the second circle. This has encouraged other younger adults and environmentally conscious citizens to purchase and redevelop their own property adjacent to this newer housing. That in turn is improving retail and starting the circle of development over again. Indianapolis is doing the same with the first circle as well. In this day of high gasoline costs and rising awareness of the environmental impact of cars, this may be a city on the edge of a great idea.

You can tell a community has made significant redevelopment progress when Starbucks establishes a shop there. Starbucks is a place for those with disposable income and a few moments of leisure time.

I am starting to see this kind of redevelopment of second circles in many cities, and you don't have to be a scientist to see that this kind of redevelopment is going to accelerate in the near future as driving becomes more expensive or people choose to live more simply.

Congregations in the second circle have challenges today. Most are struggling with a mission that makes sense in their context. Long-term residents in the area have made firm decisions regarding their participation with a faith community. These communities also have a large number of transient members (about 50 percent of this housing is owner occupied.)

Finally, the third circle of a city is usually a very static community. It is still filled with fairly stable families that have settled in. These communities will soon enter into transition, but they are not quite there yet. In many of these communities the settlers have been in their houses for twenty years or longer. Many are now retired. Their houses are in good condition, and the lawns are nice. But the houses are small compared to today's standards. They do not have the closet space, open living spaces, and large bathrooms of today's newer homes.

In some cities, younger families who want to live in the area purchase a couple of these homes, tear them down and build new homes. This requires a great deal of affluence within a community. In other places people will gut a home like this and design a completely new layout, perhaps with an addition.

Homeownership in these areas is considerably higher than in the first and second circle, usually around 75 percent. The challenge for churches in these areas is that the members of the parish are usually that group of long-term settlers who are looking for stability in their lives, not change. These congregations are not real attractive to newcomers who are making large investments in their new housing.

The other challenge for congregations in these areas is that many of their members are now aging, and possibly relocating. These churches must develop new membership in the midst of a population that wants stability.

But this is an exciting time for metropolitan congregations. There are places with new possibilities, and congregations that are open to the new realities of their community can grow as a result. There are also places where people need hope, and congregations that revise their mission can begin to make a difference in the very community where they are planted, if they will do some extensive planning. Regardless, metropolitan congregations need to keep abreast of the changes around them.

The Rural and Small Town Context

America has different kinds of small towns. Some are built around agriculture, and some have another financial base, such as the government sector or retirement destinations.

For example, small towns in the "mountain West" are usually growing despite declining economies, which were once built around mining or logging are. These are now attractive communities for retirees who are tired of living in a city. While there may be some agricultural interests in these communities, they largely thrive by providing services. The situation with agricultural based small towns is entirely different.

We recently worked with a church in a small town outside of Des Moines, Iowa. The small town had been declining in population over the past few years and the congregation was struggling to make ends meet. A member of the church had become the congregation's beloved patriarch. He had given his whole life to support the church and enable its ministry over the years. That member had died in his nineties, and now the congregation had no patriarch. That member had also been the major source of financial support for the congregation, and the church had just completed a building project with a mortgage. Memberscould not see how they could continue to make loan payments, as well as get ministries going.

While our first mission was to see if a new church could start in its facility, it became apparent that this church might have a chance if it could hold on another five years. The demographics of the area, as well as our visual review of the community, showed that the urban sprawl of Des Moines was heading their way.

This is fairly typical of what we are seeing with our small towns and rural communities today. In 1960, more than 50 percent of the U.S. population lived in these areas. Today, only about 20 percent of the U.S. population lives in these types of communities.[7]

Small towns are either being absorbed in urban sprawl, declining, or growing smaller. Their economic engines are also under great stress and change, which impacts the ability of residents to continue to live there.

Let's consider the economics of small towns today. In the past a small retail core that would normally be owned by local residents would support a small town. Their economy would be based on retail or agricultural industry. The town would have an outlet for farming equipment and feed, perhaps a grain elevator, and a local bank.

Today, mechanized farming has made it possible to work the same area of land with far fewer employees. Since transportation to grain elevators is easier, there is not a need for as many as there was in the past. With the efficiencies in place, grain can be moved very quickly and sits in storage for much shorter times.

I talked with a farmer in Illinois who had just retired and was glad to be out of farming. He stated that in his life farming had changed dramatically, and now you had to be a chemist, engineer, mechanic, hydrologist, and weatherman to continue farming. He no longer felt his bachelor's degree was enough to prepare anyone for farming and believed a farmer would need at least a master's in today's climate.

He used to borrow money for his crops from the local bank. The banker was a friend of his and even attended the same church. He asked for funds, the banker knew him, and he had the capital he needed for that year's crop. Then in the 1990s a commercial bank moved into town and lured investors away from the local bank with attractive offers. He could no longer get loans from his friendly local banker because the bank no longer had enough funds to loan him.

I asked my friend about his children. None of them live in his community any longer; none of them are in agriculture. One son got a medical degree and is practicing in a neighboring city. The other son is in finance and works in the county seat town. "There were no opportunities for them here," he said, "And I feel bad for the young men and women who choose to stay here. They are often underemployed and really struggling."

The retail cores of small towns have also changed. McCook, Nebraska, used to have a vibrant downtown community, with a lot of small businesses owned by local residents. Wal-Mart moved into the town in the early 1990s, and within ten years half of the local businesses were forced to close. While the Wal-Mart brought people in from neighboring communities and broadened the city's tax base, local businesses could not compete. A churchgoer in the community told me that shopowners couldn't buy their goods for the prices that were offered at Wal-Mart.

Sometimes a small community will gain a light manufacturing business that provides new jobs. The smaller the community, the more impact these kinds of businesses will have. The fortunes of everyone will rise and fall on these businesses. This has been demonstrated over and over again in Indiana, where the auto industry is packing up and leaving small communities. They take the community's financial base with them when they leave, and what is left are struggling businesses, people, and of course congregations.

Churches can succeed even in this climate—but it is difficult. The tenure rates of residents in these communities are very long. Many have lived in the community for several generations. They have made firm decisions about their religious affiliation and church life. They have little interest in changing that, unless there is conflict in the church or a new pastor who has "way out" ideas. These communities also have a high fall-out rate among young adults. Another issue is that outdoor recreation is highly valued by participants in these communities. You couple that with attitudes of the younger generation regarding spirituality, and you have a major loss in participation.

Churches that flourish in these kinds of communities today are those that meet a wide number of needs. Unlike a church in a metropolitan area that must pick a unique target and do very well, rural congregations must cast a wide net and provide a wide range of quality programs to sustain their ministries. Most rural communities mistakenly assume that young adults will all leave their community and do little to accommodate the next generation. Rural congregations must develop three new congregational leaders for every one they hope to retain in the future.

Essential Knowledge to Know about Your Community

One night in Long Beach, California, I was asking leaders of a congregation if they could tell me how many people lived in their area. After defining the area, I was amazed at how far off people can be. The low estimate was 30,000 people; the high estimate was 80,000 people. The census data showed 300,000 people. I asked them to guess what percentage of their population was Hispanic; their guesses were 30 to 70 percent. It was only 3 percent. The leaders could not say much about the population in the community in which they lived. They couldn't guess how many owned homes, how much people made, whether they were college educated, or anything.

A good church knows their context. Today tons of information related to your community is available on the Internet. Not all of that data makes a lot of difference for a church, however.

I have used many different sources for finding out information for congregations. Regional partners of the Christian Church (Disciples of Christ) and Church Extension, a General Unit of the Church, have made PERCEPT® data available to most congregations in our denomination. Despite this valuable resource, many churches fail to use the data, or fail to even look more broadly at their communities for their planning. Shockingly, only about 20 percent of congregations even glance at the data, let alone do anything with the information. To me, this is essential information, and any kind of planning that is done without it is very shortsighted.

I would like to suggest that the following are essential facts for churches reading a community:

- Population
- Growth rate
- Generational data about the population
- Racial data about the population
- Educational level of population
- Homeownership rate
- Household income
- Household composition (family size and composition)

Population and Growth Rates

Population figures are important for looking at your area. The issue isn't so much *how many* people live in the area, as it is related to what I like to call *witness share*. This is the number of adherents divided by the population. Depending on how you identify the psychological boundaries of your community these witness shares can vary widely.

Population/Average Worship Attendance=Witness Share
Population X .01=Witness Potential

For new church purposes, we usually look at a five-mile radius from the center of the psychological boundaries. If it is a metropolitan area, you should be able to attract .01 percent of the population to your faith community. If your church is located in a rural or small town area, that percentage can rise to 3 percent. The suburban figures range widely depending on the number of congregations in the area and the age of the community.

The formula for witness potential should yield a sustainable figure in average worship attendance. (We will cover congregational sustainability rates in the next chapter; for now, know that your formula should yield 100 or greater.)

This is not highly scientific, but it has been helpful for us in determining potential for new churches. Of course, a good church can be planted in any population and exceed these figures. This formula is just an indicator, not a hard-and-fast rule, because community and church dynamics have so many variables.

The formula changes dramatically if your racial-ethnic affinity is not a majority in a community. With the St. Louis congregation mentioned earlier in this chapter, only 20 percent of the community was Anglo. When we did the witness potential of that community (20 percent of the total population) using this formula, the congregation was actually meeting their witness potential. This sum did not project a witness share for a congregation of sustainable size.

(Population X Racial %) X .01=Witness Potential

Our goal in looking at all this information is to create sustainable ministry for our communities. This has everything to do with a congregation being relevant to its context. All this math might be somewhat daunting, but our passion in doing these equations is to encourage churches to reach their "kingdom potential" as George Bullard often states.[8] This math will come in handy when you are developing your ministry plan later.

Growth Rate

The growth rate of a community is calculated by measuring the population increase in a community during a certain period of time. Depending on that period, growth rates vary. In the United States most communities grow by 5 percent every 5 years (a little less than 1 percent per year over longer periods).

The growth rate of communities is a measurement of new population, but it is not the only measurement of new people. Population grows by families getting larger (biology) and by density increasing. You can have a community with high-rises and no conceivable place for new population that will still exceed 5 percent growth. You can also have communities with wide-open space and infrastructure in place for new housing to be built with virtually no growth rate.

A congregation I worked with in Oklahoma was convinced that their community was going to grow quickly. We took a windshield tour of the community, and they showed me block after block of new streets with sewer, water, and other services ready to go. The problem was, however, that I did not see any active construction of new homes. There were tall grass and weeds growing on every lot. The developer anticipated growth, but hadn't closed any sales. This is potential, but not realized growth.

Just because the Chamber of Commerce says a community will grow does not mean it will happen. To get an accurate measurement of growth, you need to consult the county or city building department and get a count of new residential building permits that have been filed each month compared to the previous year.

New housing units will bring new population to an area, but different types of housing will attract different people who will serve in and be served by different kinds of ministries.

Another way to measure population growth is by birth rates. Different racial-ethnic groups have different birth rates. Non-Hispanic white women have an average of 58.9 births per 1,000 women while Hispanic have 99.1 per 1,000.[9] In addition, if a community has a large number of first-generation immigrants in the area, the number of people per household will rise. This is particularly true in metropolitan areas and even small towns where workers come and go with seasonal work.

A community with stagnant population is a large challenge for a church. If the growth rate of the community exceeds 5 percent for five years, the congregation should be showing growth, if it is keeping up with its witness share. When a community is growing and the church is not, that is a reason for concern.

Another piece of data which is much more difficult to gather is the mobility rate of people in your community. This information can usually be obtained from the local school district office. It will tell you the turnover rates of classrooms and provide a hint about mobility rates in a community. The lower the mobility rate, the fewer opportunities congregations will have to welcome newcomers and make a difference in their lives. The higher the mobility rate, the more opportunities a congregation will have. The higher rate will mean also that the congregation must assimilate people more quickly and accept that participants will not always be in their church for longer periods of time.

Generational Data

I once received a call from a new congregation in Florida. This church was developed in a gated community and was meeting in the clubhouse. They were in a quandary because they were not able to attract children to participate in the Sunday school program that they were trying to develop. "You live in a restricted community, don't you?" I asked. The community would not allow anyone to live there unless they were fifty-five years of age, and children were prohibited except for short-term visits. They were reaching their demographic potential given those restrictions.

Generational information is important when looking to a congregation's future. In church development terms, we tend to divide population into two generational groups. These two groups include those who are of the Boomer generation and older (born before 1960) and the younger groups.

Not all congregations can provide an excellent witness to people of all generations. The trend is for congregations in metropolitan areas to serve specific generations well. Personally I hate to see congregations divided generationally like this, even though I understand the difficulty for congregations to serve six unique generations at one time.

I would hope for all congregations to value the ministry opportunities we have in working with children, youth, and young adults. These generations are particularly open to working with faith formational issues. I think that churches do their best work with younger populations. Unfortunately, I see many congregations doing little to accommodate these generations.

Racial-Ethnic Data

I have read and listened to many vision statements of both new and existing congregations. I have yet to read a statement that excludes any racial-ethnic group from being a part of the congregation. In many cases I have read statements where the church claims at the outset that it will become a multicultural congregation. That often fails to happen. Today the worship hour is still "the most segregated hour in this nation," as Martin Luther King, Jr. once said.[10]

The issue of race in America is very complex. Not all cultural groups share the same beliefs and values, even within their group. For example, it is wrong to assume that all Spanish-speaking congregations have the same values. I have Hispanic friends who are patiently teaching me some of the nuances between groups. My Puerto Rican colleagues grumble every time an Anglo assumes they like tacos because they speak Spanish. My Chinese friends have the same reaction when someone suggests they eat sushi.

Within the Hispanic context there are at least twenty-eight unique groups. Within the Asian context there are even more. Even among the Chinese people in America, there are thirty-eight different ethnic groups with different traditions, foods, and culture. And all that is in addition to individual differences.

Not all Hispanics speak Spanish. When people first immigrate to the United States, they have a different set of needs than people who have lived here for generations. For example, it is not unusual in Texas or New Mexico to meet a family that has lived in a specific community for many more generations than any of the Anglos that now make that area their home.

Racial-ethnic data becomes important when the group in the congregation assessing itself falls below 50 percent in the community. The statistics also must be checked against historical data. For example, if a community was 80 percent Anglo ten years ago, and today the community is only 51 percent Anglo, it indicates a significant shift in population that will likely continue. A congregation would be wise at these points to consider ways in which they can adapt to the changing dynamics of the community.

In the same way, an increase in a specific racial-ethnic group could be pointing toward a ministry opportunity. The problem is that most congregations do not know how to relate to these growing populations. However, most denominations have leaders in those racial-ethnic communities who are willing to help develop new ministries.

It has been my joy these past few years to participate in multicultural worship as we train new church pastors. With no majority group, we have borrowed the best of all cultures and experienced some powerful worship moments. It is my wish that all who profess Christ will experience what God can give us through such worship.

Educational Levels

A leader of a congregation in my community was lamenting that her congregation didn't seem to be able to attract people in their changing community. "People come, but they don't stay," she said. I knew the congregation well and I had worshiped with them on Sunday. When we began to study the educational levels of people in the community we could see a large gap.

The congregation was very "heady." They had a very sophisticated style of worship that people with a long history of church would appreciate. They also had music that was difficult to sing, and the sermon, which called us toward peace and justice, would not resonate with people whose largest concern was their inability to relate to their teenage children.

Educational levels are important. It's not that any church would purposefully exclude people of lower education levels, but socially people tend to gravitate toward people of similar education levels.

In a meeting with a group of college-educated leaders, I asked them to guess how many people in the United States had a college degree or higher. I heard figures ranging from 50 to 70 percent. They were thinking about all of the people they knew, and all of them had a college education. The reality is that in America today, only 25 percent have completed college or have a graduate degree.

We must never assume that people without the benefit of a college degree are not smart. There is nothing further from the truth, for there are different forms of intelligence. It is simply a cultural difference, and if you look at the circles of friends you have, they likely have a similar if not identical education level.

Ministry planning must take educational levels into account, especially in the design of worship and educational ministries.

Homeownership

"Over the past few years, we've seen the population of our community grow very rapidly," a pastor said. "They built large apartment complexes all around us…yet our church has yet to attract a single person from any of those places."

When we work with smaller congregations, we find that church participants are largely homeowners. Sure, the bank may own their home, but they are making mortgage payments. They are people who have put their roots down in a community, and are working to pay it off in the next twenty-five years.

Homeowners are a subculture. They watch the "Home" channel on cable TV. They shop regularly at hardware stores. They work to decorate and maintain their homes and it is important to them that their community is a safe, quality place to raise their families. For some the church becomes their "third place." That means that the church is the place they drop their kids off for scouting, music lessons in the children's music program, Bible study and worship, and some "fellowship" opportunities with other church members.

People who do not own homes do have some of the same hopes and concerns, but they are more mobile. They know if their community gets bad, they can leave. Most have nontraditional families and actually feel left out by many church activities. They develop other places for socialization with other transient members of the community, like a Starbucks coffee shop or the local pub.

Homeownership rates are good indicators of the type of ministry a church will have to offer in its community. The fewer homeowners, the more important it is to offer the kinds of experiences that will attract nontraditional families.

I had a complaint several years back from a congregation that was nesting a new immigrant congregation: "They don't take care of their kids. They get to church, and the kids just run wild!" This suburban congregation of mostly homeowners was not considering the context in which these children were living. Children that grow up in apartments are taught very early on to "be quiet" and not disturb others living in close quarters. In many of these apartments, there is very little floor space.

Children growing up in apartments will run at church. They are going to make noise as they feel more comfortable in the building. Unlike their suburban counterparts who have space outside to run, apartment kids have to wait until they are in a public space to run.

Churches must plan for ministry very differently if there is a low percentage of homeownership in their community. At this writing the United States is experiencing a decline in homeownership, with people losing their homes in record numbers. If the mortgage market tightens it will become more important for congregations to seek new ways of relating to its community.

Income Levels

Household family income is another determining factor when congregations are considering their future ministry. Household income determines a lot about the depth of engagement a family may have with a congregation.

Low-level incomes sometimes reflect a household that is engaged in the service industry, which may mean that the family has erratic work schedules and shifts. It may also be an indicator of how much free time a family has.

It is interesting to note that the fewer choices a group has within our culture, the more deeply they will engage with their congregation. The more choices a group has within our culture, the less likely they will engage heavily with the congregation, and they will demand higher quality programming to meet their needs or they will "choose" another congregation.

I was working with a first-generation Haitian congregation in Connecticut a few years back. It was a late Friday evening, and I had just finished meeting with the pastor and a few congregational leaders trying to recover their losses from a recent fire at their church (in which they lost everything). When we finished at about 8:30 p.m., I tried to excuse myself so I could get to a hotel and sleep a few hours before another early morning flight.

"Why, you can't leave yet!" the pastor said. "We are having church at 10:00 p.m., and I told everyone you would be our guest preacher."

This caught me totally by surprise, but was not unusual in our work with new congregations, so I stayed.

At 10:00 the service started. The singing and prayers lasted until about 11:30 p.m. as the congregation continued to fill the church. I was amazed at the participation at that late hour *on a Friday night!* This wouldn't happen in a suburban Anglo congregation.

A friend of mine explained the dynamics involved. The people of this church work in the hotel and service industry. Most do not get off work until 9 or 10 in the evening. They also do not have entertainment at home in their small apartments and they have little money. They have few choices, and the church really sustains them in this new foreign place. They cannot wait to worship only once on Sunday morning. Congregations such as these make a profound difference in the lives of the people they serve.

Higher income levels are challenging to work with because the people have so many choices for activities and the leisure time to engage in them. These opportunities for travel or recreation are usually selected over church participation.

When I was a church planter in the Seattle suburbs, I lived in an area with the second highest average household income in the metropolitan area. By the time our church reached sixty people in average worship attendance, I was made aware that three families were multimillionaires.

Ministry programming in this context is highly complex. Wealthy people work long and hard hours, and they have many opportunities for recreation. Congregations in these settings have to hit a fine balancing point of adequate programming and quality worship.

Household Composition

Traditional families as the twentieth-century church usually defined them are no longer the norm in many communities. This has a tremendous impact on how we think and talk about church programs. Even how we speak of the church "family."

Family structures in the United States are changing dramatically, and it has happened in a very short period of time. Consider the shift shown below:[11]

Type of Household	1973	1998
Children living with both biological parents	73%	51%
Households composed of married couples with children	45%	26%

According to the U.S. Census Bureau, in 2000 9.7 million Americans were living with an unmarried, different sex partner, and 1.2 million were living with a same-sex partner. That means 11 percent of unmarried partners are same-sex couples.[12] Also, 41 percent of American women between the ages of fifteen and forty-four have cohabitated at some point in their life.[13]

The number of unmarried couples living together increased 72 percent between 1990 and 2000, and the number increased tenfold between 1960 and 2000.[14] Also, 41 percent of unmarried partner households have children under eighteen living with them.[15] In addition, 33 percent of all births are to unmarried women.[16] This explains why 40 percent of children are expected to live in a cohabiting household at some point in their lives.[17]

As of the year 2000 the most common household type in the United States is people living alone. For example, 27 million households are made up of one person, compared to 25 million households in which there is a husband, wife, and child. In sum, an adult living alone composes 25 percent of all households. These statistics demonstrate that there are few norms for the term "traditional American Family".

Most churches use these statistics to point out the decay of our society; I am just using them to name a condition. Families in the United States are changing, and so are attitudes toward marriage, family, and divorce. The church can sit on the sidelines and judge our neighbors, or we can learn how to provide ministry for the majority of households in our community.

These changing trends are due to many issues. First, the average age of people marrying for the first time is climbing. In 1950, a man would marry at age twenty-two. Today the average age for males is twenty-seven.

Economics also have played a big part. After a church meeting one warm night, the pastor of the congregation and I walked outside the church to say our good-byes. Outside we met a really nice elderly couple in their eighties holding hands, sitting in the porch swing outside the church building. After making a joke about whether their parents knew they were holding hands, I asked, "How long have you been married?" They replied, to my surprise, "Who says we're married?"

As we walked away the pastor explained: "They've been living together for about eight years. Everyone in the church knows it, and is happy for them. If they were to marry, she would lose the survivor's benefits from her late husband's pension. We all understand it doesn't make sense for them to get married."

Young couples feel the same thing. The average student loan for a public, four-year college is $26,119.[18] It is estimated that 69 percent of students get a loan of some size. Many wait to pay off loans before marriage, pushing back the time in which they engage in family life.

The type of family structure has everything to do with ministry planning. Children growing up in single-parent homes need additional influences and support for their well-being, and churches are in a unique position to offer that kind of support. Single parents also need help. The day-to-day pressures on a single mother or father are tough, especially for single parents living in communities far away from their extended families.

The number of grandparents raising their grandchildren is also growing. Some of these grandparents are also single, taking on roles that demand tremendous energy. I have witnessed churches that have been very helpful in making a difference in the lives of these young people.

Finally, blended families and blended households are a growing trend. It is not uncommon for single parents with children to move back home with their parents. Nor is it unusual for two unrelated households to share a home for a short period of time.

Household composition gives your congregation important hints about ministry opportunities for your ministry planning.

Community Types and Ministry Types

City planners have a scientific method for determining types of communities by a select group of criteria. They measure them using four dimensions.

First, they determine if it is a suburban or urban community by homeownership, percentage of the population without a car, population density and diversity, and finally the number of single-family housing units.

Second, city planners measure the professional status level compared to poverty in a community. They look at education levels, occupations, household income, and the value of housing or the monthly rental rates.

Third, they consider the linguistics of the community. They look at what percentage of residents are English speaking/native born compared to those who are not.

Finally, they look at families. Of the nontraditional families, they want to know how many are single younger adults compared to female-headed families with children.[19]

These dimensions categorize communities by ten basic neighborhood types. On the next page I suggest the ministry opportunities that work best with each neighborhood group.

Conclusion

Demographics mean nothing unless you begin to think about the ministry opportunities that these numbers represent. *It is not about "how many?" but about "what difference can our church make?"*

As you review this chapter, you can see three ways in which we learn about a community: (1) Ask people, (2) review data on the community, and (3) observe. These are the different facets on our prisms as we reflect on a community. You have to do all three if you are going to look at your context with any sense of reality.

The balanced use of all three forms of inquiry will yield a picture of your community. If you review data without actually looking at the community, you can get a skewed view of the dynamics at work in that place. If you just drive around and look at people without talking to them, you will not discover what is motivating them. If you just talk to people without looking at data, you get a picture of their bias, but not the community.

For more ideas about how to reach your community and the benefits of such research, download and read the "Know-Your-Community" PDF on the *From Our Doorsteps* product page of www. ChalicePress.com.

As you learn about your community, think about the worldview of the people you are meeting. What is it going to cost a person to follow Christ? What does this culture think about church and Christianity? What is going to be the best delivery system for the church's ministries?

When you take a close look at a community, the ministry opportunities begin to drop in your lap. This is a much better way to do ministry planning than the standard "go to a workshop and attempt to repeat someone else's success." Relevant ministry develops a healthy congregation. Spending prayerful time discerning your community is imperative in good ministry planning.

Neighborhood Type	Ministry Opportunities
1. Very urban, impoverished, English speaking, with many female-headed families with numerous children.	Mission oriented congregation with outside sources of income. Children's programming for working mothers, job placement programs, etc. Multiple worship opportunities at different times.
2. Somewhat impoverished, mostly English speaking, with some female-headed households, located near type 1.	Same opportunities listed above, empowerment of local volunteers to engage in services. Worship and Bible study opportunities.
3. Somewhat urban, somewhat linguistically isolated. Mostly blue collar and somewhat ethnic congregations.	Racial-ethnic appropriate ministry, language classes, individual help for new immigrants and networking with the community. English and language appropriate worship and study opportunities.
4. Very well-off neighborhood with many non-family households. Usually associated with a university or higher education context.	Artistic and creative worship done with high quality. Traditional classroom discussion groups on complex topics of theology and society.
5. Urban impoverished, linguistically isolated area.	Ministry typical of home country and style of worship and language. "Bridge people" who help others relate to the broader context.
6. Very urban and very isolated community, with non-family households.	This area is usually very migratory in terms of its population. Ministry opportunities are in high demand during cultural holidays. A need for "bridge connection" with home country church. Ministry is related to comfort. Need for outside sources of financial support. Need for basic needs, i.e., food bank and clothing.
7. Urban, very well off, great many non-family households, numerous very young, unmarried adults.	Opportunities for nontraditional people with leisure time. Need for creative—nontraditional opportunities. Social service opportunities. "Emergent style of worship" works well in these kinds of communities.
8. Suburban, middle class, traditional families, mostly blue collar, some college.	The usual traditional church programs and worship styles work well here. Opportunities for children and youth programs very important. Recreational and sporting congregational programs work well in this context.
9. Suburban, well off. More prosperous suburbia.	A difficult atmosphere. Programs must have a point to them to gain participation. Counseling programs a plus as well as quality children's and youth programs offered simultaneously. Commuter congregations must limit program times.
10. Very suburban, very wealthy, highly prosperous suburbs.	The most difficult atmosphere for ministry. Residents have many, many choices in every arena of life. Quality worship and programs in a quality facility are required.

Questions for Discussion

1. When we consider our church location today, what are the psychological boundaries to our north, south, east, and west?
2. How would you describe the predominant people group our church consistently attracts?
3. Is our church near a freeway? How does that impact our congregation?
4. Where would you say our community is in terms of its life-cycle? Is it on the growth side or decline side? How old is our community?
5. What kind of impact do you feel the community's age has on our congregation?
6. Note the ten neighborhood types. Which type would best describe our situation?
7. Would our congregation benefit from more in-depth study of our context? Should we consider getting a consultant or doing a self-study?

3

Assessing Congregational Readiness

An image starts to emerge through our binoculars. The light has passed through the large objective lens, which is our macro view of our context. The light has passed through the first prism, where we reflected on our community context. If we were to end here with our analysis of the image before us, we could not see a thing, as the image would have been completely reflected back to its source.

We need a second prism in order to bring that image back toward our eyepiece. This is our reflection on our congregation, a realistic view of what the church can accomplish.

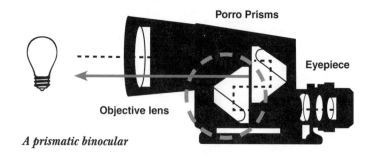

A prismatic binocular

Many ministry planning processes begin with assessing the congregation; other processes have a cursory view of the immediate context. I believe that we have to start with the larger image, looking at ministry opportunities, before we look at the congregation. Ministry planning is not about meeting the needs of the congregation, but meeting the call that God has given us to be the church. That begins by looking broadly, then focusing.

Most planning processes break down because people do not consider what is realistic for their congregation. They attend a conference at some megachurch, and come home hoping to replicate what that church did. Jim Griffith, a giant in new congregation development, calls this the "Willow-Back-Rez-Hill-Village-House-Ship-Point" syndrome.[1] Soon these enthusiastic folks are confused about why the new approach added little to their congregation.

A church in Texas went to a seminar at Willow Creek in Illinois. While there they became enamored with the "seeker service" concept, in which drama was used to introduce themes and issues related to living and faith. They bought some books and scripts, bringing them home to use on their congregation with the hope that the church would explode with growth.

There were several problems: (1) the congregation were all in their seventies and eighties, (2) there were no actors in the congregation and no one who could memorize a small script, and (3) it just looked goofy for the older participants to be talking about issues related to young adults, such as how to deal with the stress of the baby. Needless to say the "drama" only lasted several weeks before they pulled the plug and went back to their old way of being church.

Before we chuckle too much at this congregation's expense, the same scenario has occurred in church after church trying to launch a contemporary worship service without the talent to launch it.

The problem is, we try things, they fail, and we sweep it under the rug for fifteen years until we gain the courage to try something new. The point of good ministry planning is to clearly see what the congregation can do well *in its context!*

One of the reasons that Willow Creek has been such a success is because of the community in which it is a part. They are located in an area with high population density and few church participants. This is not Texas. Nor is the Saddleback Church in Texas, or the Crystal Cathedral. The dynamics of each and every community play directly into what your church is called to be.

I have a son who is a missionary in China. Some fellow faculty members asked him to travel to another city and be a judge for an English competition. He agreed and traveled eight hours to the city.

He was in a completely foreign environment and was immediately put on stage in front of hundreds of Chinese university students who began numerous presentations in English. He was not given any criteria, or a list of student names, or any idea of how many presentations he would be listening to. He was just expected to know how to assess the contestants.

Before we can begin to evaluate a congregation, we need some common understanding about what a vital congregation looks like. We must have some idea about what they are doing and how they accomplish ministry, or the process is awkward. We do not just instinctively know how well-positioned our congregation is for mission.

Several years ago coworkers Lori Adams, Bill Bass, and I met at my home to study vital congregations through the works of our church development heroes. We had just spent time reading the works of Lyle Schaller, George Bullard, Bill Easum, Ed Stetzer, Dick Hamm, Nancy Ammerman and countless others to see what they thought about vital congregations.

We came up with a list of more than thirty significant factors that these insightful people had pointed to as signs of vital congregations. We then grouped the list into subgroups, and were finally amazed to see that all the factors listed by these writers fit into four rather neat categories. The result was a list of "Four Marks of a Vital Congregation."

1. A clear and compelling mission and vision that is driven by the Gospel.
2. Contextual relevance to the community in which they are called to serve
3. Passion and energy for meeting that mission
4. Resources (human and financial) and the ability to mobilize those assets for the mission

1. A Clear and Compelling Mission and Vision That Is Driven by the Gospel

When you visit Pendleton Christian Church in Pendleton, Indiana, a group of people who are clear about who they are and what God has called them to be will greet you. This congregation has grown from an average of just 60 in worship to multiple services that average more than 500. They accomplished this in just a few years in a small community that is only growing slightly.

Their pastor is Rev. Michael Canada, a former basketball player who preaches barefooted. When he first came to the congregation, he learned the lay of the land, looked at his community, and discovered that while the people in his church were wonderful, they had no unifying idea of their mission. The church was doing all kinds of different things, with little sense of purpose or direction.

After his first year he was pretty depressed. The church had grown slightly, but the people of the congregation seemed to have a lot of different ideas about how the church should act. He spent time in study and reflection, and then, while on study leave in Dallas, he went to the Potter's House for worship. During that time he heard a powerful sermon by T.D. Jakes.

The message he heard that day was based on the healing of a paralytic. Jesus is teaching in a wealthy man's home when some men bring their friend who is paralyzed on a stretcher to be healed. However, there were so many people in the home they could not get near Jesus. So they went on the roof, tore a hole in it, and lowered the man in front of Jesus, who healed him.

The sermon point was that the church should be like the rich man who owned the house where Jesus taught because that man was willing to let strangers tear a hole in his roof so that someone could get closer to Jesus.

That became the vision for the Pendleton church. As the church plans and provides ministry, they ask themselves "Are we being faithful to our vision of a church that is willing to let someone put a hole in our roof so someone can get closer to Christ?" When you meet people in the church, there is no sense of propriety or ownership; the congregation is willing to sacrifice their time, resources, and energy so that someone can get closer to Jesus.

This is a welcome contrast to congregations that are failing. The stories are legion: A congregation will not allow the youth to paint a room in the church because it wouldn't fit the décor of the church building. A congregation won't nest a Korean congregation because they don't want the smell of their food lingering in the building. A congregation won't consider letting some young adults bring a drum set into the sanctuary to present a few contemporary worship songs.

The vision of a church that allows the roof to be torn off is a powerful way to engage the Gospel with a compelling vision for the future of the church. That is why we intentionally state that the Gospel must drive the vision and mission of a congregation.

I have read hundreds of vision statements written by different church leaders. They usually lack the compelling element because they are so broad in scope and do not lead to anything that a person wants to give their time towards. Usually they are not driven by the Gospel.

One such congregation was a new church on the east coast. The vision for this congregation was to provide a place of worship for Disciples of Christ people who lived in that particular community. The vision is asking people to give of themselves for the purpose of helping a group of pre-selected people who live in a community. As you can imagine, this congregation failed to take root, and the congregation closed within two years. People in the postmodern world are not compelled to give themselves for the sake of an institution. That is not what Jesus gave his life for either.

A vision statement is a compelling statement about the congregation's attitude as they work toward their future mission. It states what the fruits of that mission will look like when the congregation is faithful to the vision.

Just knowing the attitude through which your church is going to work toward the future is not enough. The congregation must have a clear sense of their own identity. Working with new congregations has given me a tremendous respect for this single concept. Our team has trained more than 700 new church planters and their core team members. We know that those who can best articulate their vision, mission, and values are going to excel in church planting.

You see, when a congregation is new, the vision, mission, and values are all they have for identity. The new church has no building, no offering plates, no resources, no funds, just identity statements about who they are, who they want to serve, what their needs are, and what they are going to do about it.

A congregation must have a target for their passion. That is why a mission statement must be added for the clarity of a congregation's identity.

A mission statement is a statement about who the congregation hopes to serve, what the needs of the people to be served are, and what the congregation members are going to do.

Dr. Jacques Nicholas is pastor of Good Shepheard Christian Church in North Miami, Florida. This new congregation clearly identified first-generation Haitian immigrants as the people they felt called to serve. Nicholas, himself an immigrant, had a vision that they would eventually serve as many as 10,000 people in Florida, and he has a congregation that already numbers in the hundreds.

I have been to Haiti and have seen the context people in his church left. Everything in Haiti is broken, nothing works, power is sporadic, water is not dependable, yet the people there have a wonderful spirit.

Nicholas knew the needs of people in his church. Immigration issues are complex and difficult for Haitians in the United States, and the demand for help is very high. Many also have financial, language, and other kinds of needs as well. And more than anything, there is a need for people like Nicholas to bring their positive attitudes from Haiti as they deal with American culture.

Nicholas knew that his church could grow and serve the needs of people by providing a lot of small-group experiences and contact. He understood that as people develop relationships with each other and begin to trust and pray for each other, they will help each other out in the most appropriate ways. And so they have.

I worshiped with this congregation in its early days. They were meeting in a public storage facility in a very long, narrow garage–yet the people overflowed to the parking lot. It was hot, humid, and late at night when I worshiped with them at a 10:00 p.m. service. I was cautioned to not preach too long because they had a midnight service to get ready for. During the service the small group leaders would stand and report about the past week's meetings. They would list prayer concerns for the community and report the ways in which God had answered prayers in the lives of the people who were around them. I could only hear spotty reports from my translator, but it was powerful.

This is a congregation that knew who God had called them to serve and had a method for meeting those persons' needs. You will note that the ministry was not all dependent on the pastor, but employed a method by which the entire congregation was engaged in serving one another and the people in their community.

Without clarity of purpose, a church can be going in too many different directions. We frequently work with congregations that are trying to provide ministry for every group of people in their community. While this is admirable, it is not an effective focus of energy. Churches need to focus their energy on what they can do best, and a well-written mission statement will get everyone on the same page.

A church in Arizona was dealing with this dynamic. One group of people felt the best thing the church could do was host a rummage sale. Another group felt they needed to reach out to the growing Hispanic population in their community. Another group felt that the church should be a place of fellowship. It all came to a head one Sunday when the congregation attempted to have a luncheon in the fellowship hall while a Hispanic congregation worshiped in the sanctuary, and they had no place for their children because all the classrooms were full of rummage.

Without clarity of purpose, people can work at cross-purposes. Some will work at change, while others work to keep things the same. The result is a congregation of people who have energy to do something, but cannot choose what to do.

Finally, congregations need to be clear about their values.

While serving a new congregation in Seattle some years ago, we developed a whizbang church school program. Part of what made that effective was that in the early development stages of that program, we listed several clear values about it, which gave parents some clarity about what their children would be learning in our church school.

One of those values was that "we will not scare children into faith." That is to say, we intended to teach Christ, not the devil. I know some of my readers will not agree with that value, but we felt God was calling us toward that principle as we developed this important program. Our parents knew these values, and so did our teachers.

One afternoon I got a call from a parent who was angry. "I feel like you guys are abusing my trust," she said. Her six-year-old son, who had an active imagination, could not sleep at night because our teacher had told him he had to be right with God or Satan would get him. She asked me: "Did our values as a church change somewhere and I wasn't told about it?"

I had the fun job of calling the teacher to ask for his input on this situation, at which time he challenged this basic value of our program. It wasn't our best moment, but we had to stand for our values as a church. If he challenged this basic value, how many others would he challenge in the future? We lost a good member, but our church could not compromise its programs for the sake of keeping him engaged.

This man went to another congregation that had no set of clearly stated values, and he created numerous issues for several years for that congregation, which eventually led to the resignation of the pastor.

Value statements are a small list of biblical and theological principles that the congregation holds without compromise.

A simple value statement for a Disciples congregation is that we believe in an open Communion table. We have no tests for participation except our profession of faith in Jesus Christ.

These values are helpful for new participants who are considering being a part of your church. If they know these values, and why the congregation chose them, it helps them decide their level of participation with a congregation.

However, the list has to be short. No one wants to be a part of a congregation with dozens of dogmatic statements that control their lives. Short and simple is the hallmark of congregational identity.

2. Contextual Relevance

A contextually relevant congregation offers services that will reach enough people in their community in a way that will enable their ministry to be self-sustaining. That means they are providing services for a large enough "people group" in their community that will lead the congregation to sustainability.

Vital congregations are answering the questions that people are actually asking in their community. They understand their community and the people who live there. They also understand a need to be flexible in order to meet new ministry opportunities.

I worked with a fifteen-year-old congregation that now only averages fifteen in worship. Five years ago the church, which had up to thirty people in worship then, moved into a beautiful new facility at their new site. The people in the congregation came from the nearby city and several other suburbs ten to fifteen miles away. Nobody in the church actually lived in the community in which they built their sanctuary.

After five years in their new building they couldn't understand why the people who lived in the community were not attending. As I met with the key leaders, I asked them about their neighbors. The response was a very uncomfortable silence, as no one in the room had ever even talked with one of the neighbors except the man who mowed the grass for them.

The reality was that this community was depressed economically, with run-down homes, high unemployment, a declining retail core, and little hope. The congregation was in a brand new building, with members who drove nice cars and who wouldn't even eat lunch in the local diner because it didn't look too appetizing. The congregation had bought the land because it was a good price. The congregation was like an absentee owner in a place where the Gospel could make a large difference in the lives of those around them.

A congregation in northern California understood this concept after many years of not grasping it. This church was once a focal point for all Disciples in northern California, as it was located two blocks from the Pacific Ocean; it was the place of many summer revivals in the 1930s. As time progressed the church failed to adapt to the changing community and had dropped to just thirty in worship. The congregation was trying to be faithful to its traditions, which meant less and less to people near them. They were a good church, but placed in the wrong place for that kind of witness.

A year ago the congregation developed a new ministry plan that explored in detail the people in their community. The plan included excerpts from interviews with new residents, their attitudes about church, and their attitudes about faith. Immediately after the congregation enacted their new plan, the church began to grow, and within a year has more than doubled in worship size. A letter from a former member stated: "there are all kinds of people engaged in this church now. I would not have given this church a chance of ever making this transition just two years ago."

3. Passion and Energy

I visited a church where the congregation and pastor were totally burned out. Worship started late because the leaders were dragging in late. (As a visitor I had arrived early and had to wait fifteen minutes in the parking lot!) The lay leader who was giving the call to worship started by saying, "Well, I guess it's time we start," and things went downhill from there.

The music was slow, and only a few members stood to sing, while most remained sitting, not even looking at the words in the hymnal. The announcements (reading everything that was printed in the bulletin on the church calendar for the week) took fifteen minutes of the service. Only two things were happening that week, but it still took fifteen minutes. The prayer time was by rote. A soprano soloist tried to spice things up a bit by singing an upbeat song with recorded accompaniment, but the sound guy was off drinking coffee when it was finally her time to sing. When the pastor began to preach by reading his manuscript, I wanted to take his pulse to make sure he was alive.

When worship was over, however, it was a different church. It was like people woke up. They knew how to socialize, joke, and welcome the stranger. They just were not very enthusiastic about their faith, and a little nervous about showing passion in worship.

I was raised in the Calvinist tradition. We were highly skeptical of people who had passion and energy. Worship was meant to be done in our heads, not necessarily in our hands and hearts. We were steeped in the notion that music was to be slow and plodding, and that any demonstration of emotion was unsightly.

Many churches feel that same way, and unfortunately none of us would say they are vital congregations. We rarely question why we have adopted this way of being. The same people in these kinds of congregations are capable of showing passion. After all, they likely go to the football game and cheer, dance, scream, do the wave. (I am looking forward to getting the wave sometime when I am preaching... that would be fun!)

I was a classically trained organist. My undergraduate degree was in music, and my instrument was the pipe organ. Most pipe organs (other than tracker systems) have a slow response to the touch. From the moment you depress the key until the pipe speaks there is a gap. If you are listening to the congregation sing while you play, the hymn will get slower and slower. This issue, plus Queen Victoria's dislike of rhythm in churches, led us to the notion that music was to be slow and rhythm less.

Later in life I learned that Martin Luther, composer of "A Mighty Fortress Is Our God" actually wrote the hymn as a madrigal, not a dirge like most churches sing it.

I believe that a congregation can be intellectually stimulating, true to the Gospel, and highly effective while showing emotion and passion. In the postmodern world it will be difficult to motivate participants in a congregation without some depth of passion and energy. Contemporary worship is not the only style that leads to this passion. Congregations that worship in traditional styles can do so with passion and energy.

Vital congregations have a high level of enthusiasm. They walk with purpose in worship. They are excited about the ways in which God answers prayer. They have a fire and a spirit where Christ is seen in them, and they are thrilled to welcome the new disciple. They are also committed to helping people mature in their faith, not just getting them to make a confession, but to grow as a result of their decision.

4. Resources and the Ability to Mobilize Them for Mission

I worked with a congregation that had lots of financial resources. Some years ago a wealthy member of the church created a trust fund of nearly $2 million. This trust pays the congregation about $80,000 per year. The congregation also has a good facility that is worth about $2 million and is in a very densely populated area. The church's parking lot grossed $60,000 in rental fees last year, and they are in conversation with a cell phone company about a tower on their property. You would think that congregation had it made.

The truth is that while the congregation has financial resources, it does not have human resources. The congregation averages about twelve to fifteen people on Sundays, and the only person who has a job is the pastor, who is bi-vocational.

Resources are a lot more than just money. Resources are volunteers, leaders, a building or site for ministry, and finally money.

Congregational Resources
• Leaders
• Volunteers
• Facilities
• Finances

A building can be a tremendous resource for ministry, but it can also be a huge problem. A church in Seattle has a building of nearly 30,000 square feet, located in one of the hottest real estate markets in the United States. However, it is much more space than the congregation needs. This congregation of sixty in worship spends an enormous amount of their finances and a lot of their volunteer hours on maintaining that facility. Built in 1920, the building is so costly for their resources that they have little left to provide ministry, thus keeping the congregation in a constant circle of need.

Buildings used to their fullest potential can be an enormous resource for a congregation. Any new church planter who is working out of rental space will tell you how much they wish they could have a place in which to stage ministry and programs. Many new congregations will nearly double in size when they move into their first church building. A building can be a passive, yet effective means of attracting people into a congregation. When a church is open to the community for many different activities, it can also serve as an attraction for future prospects, as well as being a means of serving the community.

Leadership is also a valuable resource. I met with a few leaders of a congregation in Colorado that was considering closing. The church had declined to just a handful of people, most of whom were elderly and in very poor health. Only two members were in their late fifties; the rest were in their late seventies or eighties. One of the leaders requested a private meeting with me. He told me how things were working for their congregation: "They look to me for everything. I have to make the coffee, get people out of their cars and into the building, pay the bills, count the offering, and most Sundays make communion. I have a family and a demanding job. I don't know how I can continue to do this."

This man saw what a great resource *leaders* are for a congregation. Unfortunately, most congregations believe that leaders are just hatched in a congregation without any preparation or training. We do little in most congregations to actually develop future leaders. Instead, we use our current leaders over and over again until we totally use them up.

Many congregations confuse managers with leaders. There is a distinct difference between being a leader and a manager. A leader creates new visions for the future and takes a group of volunteers to a place they would not have gone otherwise. Managers, on the other hand, are people who can maintain something the way it has always been. We often say that we want leaders for certain tasks, but the reality is that if that person tries to do something different, we make it hard on them.

Usually, the person who runs the church school program is a manager. They have teachers in place on Sunday, the teachers have materials, the activities take place at the appointed time, and the manager counts how many kids came so we can have enough teachers the following Sunday.

A person who *leads* a church school program creates a compelling vision for what their Sunday school could look like. They motivate people to engage in the process because it has great meaning and importance in the life of the children who will attend. They empower teachers to be creative, and offer workshops that give them the tools they need to provide meaningful educational experiences.

We will discuss managers in more detail as we look at the life-cycle of a congregation. The point here is that vital congregations make a distinction between leaders and managers and mobilize them effectively.

Finally, vital congregations have financial support for the vision they are trying to achieve. I have met a number of incredibly compassionate new church planters who have a clear vision of how a church could reach some incredibly painful human needs in some of our most needy communities. Their visions will fall short though, unless they plan for the financial resources to make it happen.

Dr. Carolyn Bibbs is an outstanding example. In 2001, Bibbs came home to find her house in Memphis had been robbed. It was not the first time. She prayed her concerns that night: "This community is going to the dogs, Lord…when are you going to send someone here to work with these kids so they can have good lives?" Her answer came to her that evening when she felt God calling her to do something for children in her community.

That was the beginning vision for Saving Station Christian Church. The vision for this congregation was to provide a congregation for children and youth that would focus on their specific needs, such as tutoring, activities, and experiences that few inner city kids would ever have, such as organized sports, summer camps, and more. This was a strong vision, a much-needed ministry, but it did not have a financial engine to run it. Most congregations receive income from adult members who have jobs and share portions of their income.

It didn't mean it was a bad idea. It just meant that Bibbs had to think of a new way to fund ministry without relying on offering income as the primary means of support. With her connections in the city, Bibbs was able to get civic leaders, civic organizations, neighboring congregations, and even grant income to support the ministry. Today this youthful congregation worships on Saturday nights in a former trucking warehouse with sixty to a hundred energetic youth. The church is making a big difference for these children and the community.

Most good ministry ideas die because people do not consider the financial implications or do not have the desire to seek additional sources of funding. Many good ministry ideas also fail because people do not consider outside sources of funding and pass over an idea because they cannot image diverse income streams.

During my thirty years of ministry I have had the joy of starting at least fourteen nonprofit organizations that have worked in mental health, human relations, and social justice issues. In every one of those cases, we did not have a dime to begin, just a compelling vision and a desire to see our community change. The funding that was needed always followed. I believe that any good vision for ministry will receive the resources that are needed for it to become sustainable. But the vision has to be shared, people must be empowered, and it has to make a difference.

Vital congregations have a way of making that happen. They have clarity about their mission and identity, they make a difference in their context, they are passionate about achieving it, and they can mobilize their resources to enable it to happen.

Congregational Life-cycle

Organizations have a life-cycle that is fairly predictable. In 1959, Mason Haire wrote a book entitled *Modern Organization Theory*.[2] He used a biological model for describing organizational growth. This concept took root in many places, but was introduced to church development concepts by Dr. Arlin Routhauge of the Episcopal Church. Other sociologists and psychologists have added to the depth of this research, such as Erik Erikson and his human development theories, Jean Piaget in moral development theory, James Fowler's work in faith development and Martin Saarinen's work in organizational development.

I would like to introduce you to life-cycle theory in a basic form, adding some observations that I have had the privilege of witnessing in congregations today.

Four basic elements are engaged in a church's development at all times. They are Energy/Vision, Intimacy, Program, and Administration. While all these elements are in place throughout a life-cycle of a congregation, one of these four dominates the life of the congregation at any one time.

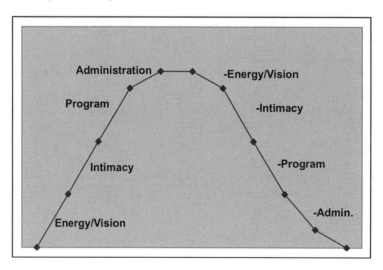

Dr. Denise Bell, senior associate pastor of Mississippi Boulevard Christian Church has a great way of explaining this. She states that all four people are on the bus, but that a different element is driving the bus at any one time.

- **Energy/Vision: (E/V)**—This element is the dreaming and creative element in an organization's life. When energy and vision are driving the bus, the church is casting a new vision for its future and is energized by the creative process.
- **Intimacy: (I)**—This element is the relational aspect of the congregation's life. When intimacy is driving the bus, the church

people are relating to one another with a high level of trust. They even like each other.

- **Program:** (P)–This element is the programmatic aspect of the congregation's life. When Program is driving the bus, the congregation is organizing its life with systems and strategies that lead to personal and corporate growth.
- **Administration:** (A)–This element is the management-organizational aspect of a congregation's life. When Administration is driving the bus, the congregation is engaged in keeping track of things, working in a "neat and orderly" fashion, and focusing on policy and process to maintain its resources and traditions.

A congregation usually starts with a small group of people who are the congregation's core leaders. The congregation then enters a period of growth and reaches a point of stability. This is the growth side of a congregation's life-cycle, and is considered to be a positive process.

Energy/Vision

A congregation or any organization begins with a compelling vision of what it can become. This vision is driving the bus. The congregation only has a vision for the future, a few people who do not know each other well, an occasional Bible study, and some rudimentary organizational stuff. This vision of an unrealized future is so compelling that it taps the energy and passion of people who desire to work toward that future. They are unified around that vision, and are committed to seeing that vision take root.

Intimacy

People who were drawn by the vision of the congregation begin to meet one another. As they do, they begin to care for one another and one another's famlies. They pray for each other, share their lives, and develop trust. As these relationships develop, the congregation is developing intimacy.

This is a powerful element in a congregation's life. People who care about one another will go to great lengths to be together. Congregational development is dependent on it. People must develop strong relationships with integrity if the congregation is going to move toward a healthy future. A lot of congregations can get stuck here. We call this dynamic "Loving each other to death." Congregations that are stuck in this phase cannot let new people into their circle because, "we don't know *them.*"

Program

Soon people who care for each other begin to note needs for programs that will help enable the development of the people they care about. In a new congregation, someone may note that several people have good voices, and they put them together in a music group, which becomes the start of a music program. A person may note that a growing number of young children would benefit from an education program. This starts informally, but then becomes a regular part of the program of the church. Before long there are Bible studies, women's groups, and youth programs.

The program is driving the bus. Everything the church does supports its overall program. Fellowship groups and even the leadership are focused on developing and organizing programs.

Administration

As the church increases its programs and has more organizational needs, it develops the structures that stabilize the "norms" of the church. This is symbolized by by-laws, budgets, and committees. Administration is now driving the bus. The purpose of these structures is not to growth, but maintaining and managing resources and people. This kind of stabilization is good while the church is growing. However, when stabilization leads to decline, it can be very problematic.

The church has an option at this point in its life-cycle. It can revise its vision and mission—which will start the life-cycle again with new energy, intimacy, and programs—or it can continue on the same path. Having maintenance as the primary driver predictably leads to decline.

Loss of Energy/Vision

If a congregation fails to "reinvent" itself, organizational matters become more important than the program life of a church. The church develops a yearly calendar that is rarely changed, and programs are offered even though there are few or no participants.

People in the church begin to lose energy, and worse yet, forget about the original vision of the church, instead serving the mechanics of being the church.

People may not leave the church at this point, but they are not attending as frequently, because they are not truly engaged as they were at the start of the life cycle.

Loss of Intimacy

As the congregation loses energy, people become less concerned about each other. Since little has changed, people's behavior becomes too predictable, and relationships in the church begin to dissolve.

When people lose their vision and energy, relationships will break down, people will fight over different opinions related to the vision of the church, or may even work at cross-purposes. As people tire and relationships break down, people will leave the church, forcing fewer leaders to do more of the work.

Loss of Program

When relationships break down, it becomes difficult to get volunteers, and thus programs begin to break down. If you think about it, why would Mrs. Smith want to teach little Billy in a Sunday school class if she no longer respected his family?

Congregations begin to reach a tipping point as relationships break down; there are no longer people who are willing to volunteer. The volunteer core gets smaller, and the church burns out its faithful participants. This fuels the loss of energy and accelerates the decline of the congregation. When a church cannot provide programs, it cannot attract and retain new participants either.

Loss of Administration

In the final stages, people begin to fight over who can vote at congregational meetings. Corporate matters are the most important thing. Concern over money and management of the few human and financial resources becomes the mission of the church. The last thing to go in a church is its legal structures, such as the by-laws

This is a sad phase in the life of a congregation. Even though we try to celebrate its ministry to a community, it is hard to see what is left of a church at the end of its life.

I went to McCook, Nebraska, a few days after that congregation had closed its ministry. The regional minister and I were looking at the building and the community to determine if it would be worth attempting to start a new congregation in the nice facility that was left by the congregation. It was a sad visit.

As we walked through the empty building we found yellowed papers with pictures drawn by Sunday school children years before. We saw a lovely decorated parlor that had housed many insightful conversations by the adult classes as people pondered their faith and spiritual growth.

In the sanctuary the Bible was opened on the pulpit to the last passage of scripture that was read to that congregation. On the piano was the last hymn that they had sung from the hymnal. And on the communion table was the dried-out bread and fermenting grape juice from the last time they shared in that communal feast. It was a painful walk, but not nearly as painful as what took place next.

We went to the home of the last officer of the congregation. She was a woman in her late seventies who had grown up in the church. She was ill and moved slowly. Over the years she had held just about every job that church had to offer. She loved the people with whom she worshiped, and when they were sick she went to their homes many times with soup, prayer, or just a pat on the back. Today we were asking her to perform the last task as the last officer of that congregation, which was to sign the title of the property over to the region. As she signed, neither the regional minister nor I could begin to imagine the pain and loss she felt at this point in her life. After years of service to this congregation, there was no one to give her soup, pray with her, or just pat her on her back.

The last element driving the bus in that church was Administration.

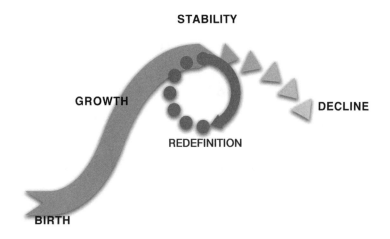

The sad part about congregations that are in decline is that they could have avoided it by revisioning their ministry. The average life span of a congregation in the United States today is about eighty years, unless the church reinvents itself. It is similar to the average life-cycle of a person. With Disciples of Christ congregations, the churches that are closing have an average life span of just over sixty-seven years.

However, many vital congregations last hundreds of years. They do so by regularly revisioning their mission and keeping true to their context. Revisioning ministry keeps a congregation from following the predictable life-cycle to its end result.

The Line of Sustainability

When you consider the life-cycle of a congregation, it is important to recognize its line of sustainability.

Congregational Sustainability is a church development term used to describe a ministry that is capable of continuing without expending outside resources or resources from a previous generation.

A long-term congregation may not be sustainable even though it is paying its bills and offering worship every Sunday. Congregations can mask sustainability by not taking care of their building. Deferred maintenance is a sign of lack of sustainability; the church cannot afford to keep its property up because they do not have the resources to sustain themselves.

Another way congregations mask sustainability is by spending their permanent funds. Congregations that dip into these reserves are depleting the congregation's total worth at alarming rates.

A congregation in Denver had done this in a serious way over the past five years. The church had a number of houses they had purchased on the property surrounding the church so they would be able to expand in the future. When the church began its decline, they opted to sell houses and live off the funds. This congregation, which averaged only fifty people on Sunday, had a full staff typical of a "program sized" congregation. They were spending 140 percent of their offering income on salaries alone.

This congregation had depleted its worth by close to $1 million in just five years by selling property to pay for operating expenses. Today the congregation has greatly reduced its staff and is reorganizing its ministry in a way that lives within their means.

Lyle Schaller's research showed that a Methodist church could sustain itself with a full-time pastor, full program, mission giving and a building with only thirty people in average worship attendance *in*

1930! He suggests that today it takes 130 people in average worship attendance to sustain a church.[3]

As I have played with this line of sustainability, I am discovering that the average worship attendance needed to sustain a congregation is different in every situation depending on the cost of living index, building size, age of construction, and other factors. Every church has a unique line of sustainability.

A new congregation is not sustainable. It has great vision and passion, but it does not have a building, a communion chalice, a nursery crib, or any of the things we associate with a church. As it develops, it reaches a point of sustainability, that is to say, if the church planter were to leave, it would survive.

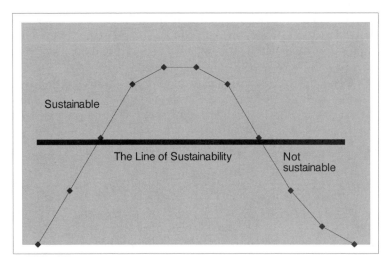

When congregations decline, they reach a tipping point where they can no longer sustain themselves. Church people are clever, however, and churches find ways to continue even though they do not have the financial means. Usually congregations control spending by lowering their giving to outside missions and by reducing their program expenditures. They have Sunday school teachers pay for their own materials, the choir sings the same anthems over and over, and the preacher can forget about a raise.

Also congregations are finding many ways to sustain themselves with outside sources of income. This would be income from cell-phone towers, rental income, and even operating day care facilities and schools.

One of our consultants visited a congregation in California that spoke with pride of their preschool as they showed the consultant the property. Within a few moments it became apparent that the preschool dominated the church. The director of the school was the only functioning church board member; the entire facility was decorated like a preschool; and the classrooms were the preschool's first, and a Sunday school class could use them *"if the church kids didn't touch anything."* When the consultant looked at the financial statements, he discovered that the preschool provided 65 percent of the congregation's operating income. The preschool was paying the pastor's salary and building expenses while the congregation's giving supported only 35 percent of the church's ministry.

This was not a ministry of the church. The church was a ministry of the preschool. There comes a point in a church's life where dependency on outside income sources or previous generational giving is just unhealthy. A sustainable congregation supports more than 65 percent of its budget with congregational giving.

Congregations can sustain themselves by using the resources of a previous generation. The question congregations must ask of themselves is if the way in which they spend their resources honors the witness of their predecessors, or if there might be some other way in which the church should consider expanding its witness.

People Types

Just as certain elements drive the bus in the life-cycle of a congregation, certain groups of people seem to have more power at different points of the church's life-cycle. There are four kinds of people in this paradigm: creative, idealistic people; relational folks; leaders; and managers.

Creative, Idealistic People

Creative, idealistic people havethe ability to think outside of the box. They are motivated by concepts and the notion of a better world. They can visualize things that are not a reality. They are very future-oriented and rarely have their own feet firmly planted on the ground. Without lots of coaching they will not always have the ability to put dreams into reality.

Relational Folks

These people have the uncanny ability to remember names and places and people, even though they only met and talked with them for a few moments. They are connected in their community by relationships and are never afraid to call in favors.

Leaders

These people have the ability to lead volunteers to a place where they would not have gone otherwise. They can cast visions, inspire people, and develop programs that make a difference in peoples lives.

Managers

Think of a store manager. They are competent, open the store at the right time, and they have staff in place, inventory on the shelf, and a system for closing at the end of the day. They are excellent at maintaining a system and can put things into place to ensure they are done continuously. They do not create new concepts, but are well grounded at keeping things going.

The church needs the gifts of all four types of individuals. However, I have observed times in a church's life when one type of individual is valued over the other. I believe this is driven largely by the place in which the church is in its life-cycle.

When a congregation first begins, it is only an idea and a vision. The start of a congregation occurs when people get together and dream. Core groups for new churches are largely made up of creative, idealistic people. This group *loves* to dream and think of better ways of being the church.

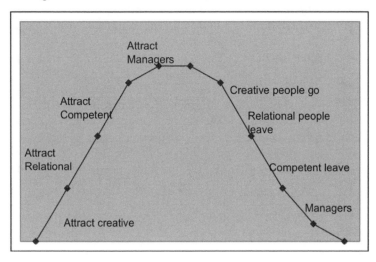

Relational people, leaders, and managers are often in that group, but they tend to put a damper on the dreaming. The managers want to take the dream and form a system that can be replicated; the relational people want to start getting people together before the church has a firm idea of its identity; and the leaders have other agendas that they want to place on the group. These kinds of people are highly frustrated during the dreaming phase and likely won't engage much. They will usually seek an established church.

In the initial stage the creative people are highly valued for their ability to dream and think outside of the box. However, the church discovers soon that they cannot dream forever, that there is a time when the church has to launch.

The next group to be given power in the congregation's life-cycle is the relational people. This group of people is highly gifted by their connectedness with the community. As the church forms and begins to launch, they suddenly realize they need some help. For example, a congregation may need someone who is a musician. That is when the relational person comes to the front of the room: "I know somebody who can do that. I will ask them if they have some interest in being our worship leader."

The relational person may or may not have anticipated the church would need a musician, but when the issue emerged, they found the person needed. The group will then ask, "Who else do you know?" Relational people are a huge asset to a congregation in this phase of development. As the church launches and new people come into the life of the church, the relational folks are greeting the stranger, learning about them, and connecting with them with ease.

Now the church is gaining momentum. It has launched, thanks to the imagination of the creative people and the connections of the relational folks. The church is still a bit chaotic, needing more groups and programs to continue to engage and help people grow in their faith. This is when the church begins to recognize the leaders in their midst and ask them to come to the front.

A church recognizes it needs a children's program and asks a leader type to put it together. This person works with a small group, develops a vision for the ministry, organizes people based on their gifts, and successfully launches a good program. The leader works with creative people to dream, but then the leader makes those dreams reality. The leader will ask the relational person for a list of names of people that could help.

During this phase of development, churches love leaders and the leaders appreciate being able to offer their gifts in a way that can make a difference. This all begins to change as the church gets more organized.

As the church develops, and leaders are expanding programs, the church realizes they need to manage what they have. They have property that needs to be cared for; they need better accounting systems in place; and they need to set up systems aimed at the congregation replicating its growth.

Managers are highly valued during this phase of development. They are particularly helpful when the church system is growing. They have the gift to see ways to organize the church's life and can put together an organizational chart, church budget, by-laws, constitutions, policies, and more.

You will note that once the managers become most valued, the congregation begins to level off. This is because a system that is replicating itself over and over again will lead to stability, not growth. A factory that is set up to produce 100 widgets a day cannot increase productivity unless more space is built or something new is introduced to the system. The same is true for a church. It cannot expand unless new programs, ideas, and classes are added. Managers are not big fans of expanding, because it creates more complex systems to manage.

The shifting power of these groups is as predictable as a congregation's life-cycle. It is truly an honor to watch these groups of differently gifted people come into the life of a congregation. I did not realize this dynamic until years of reflection on my years as a church planter. As a church planter I spent a lot of time in the initial stages of the development of the church trying to engage managers. But they had little interest in worshiping in a high school. As soon as we built the building, though, we were flooded with managers and were blessed by their participation, as long as we were growing.

Congregations decline when they fail to realize their need for more creativity in the system. This is when the congregation employs the famous seven last words of a dying church *"we've never done it that way before."* The church is so focused on managing its system that it has begun to forget why it was formed. The church believes that if it could just manage itself more, the church would begin to grow again.

Managers and creative people do not normally hang out together. They drive each other nuts. The creative people are labeled as having their heads in the clouds. Creative people see managers as unimaginative. When the managers have more power in the church system, the creative people will leave, as they sense they are no longer valued.

As a new church begins, the creative people have seen their dream realized, and they begin to get restless. They offer new ideas, which are often rejected by the managers because they do not appreciate creative new ways of messing with the system that they have put into place. But creative people hate "walking the dog." That is to say, they get bored with an order of worship that has been the same for the past seventeen years, with the same music, the same faces, etc.

At this point the church system lacks the gifts creative people add to the mix. The church recognizes a need for new ideas, and the managers organize retreats for dreaming, but those retreats only produce ideas or ways of tinkering with the system, not adapting it for the kind of community in which the church is now a part.

Now the managers tighten the system. The first thing they reduce is fellowship opportunities, and they stop paying for cookies at the coffee hour. They turn the nursery over to volunteers and recruit the relationally gifted people for tasks that take them away from the larger group.

The relational people were attracted to the church originally because of the energy of the creative people. With that group leaving, the relational people soon realize that their gifts are not really appreciated. Especially since they were stuck in the nursery the last four Sundays. The church has taken away their favorite things, and they are finding themselves with fewer reasons to go to church on Sunday. They love the people at the church, but they have a huge appetite for meeting new people, and the church is no longer attracting them. So the church begins to lose the relational people.

This is a tipping point, as it begins to accelerate the decline. The managers tighten up the system even more, accelerating the decline. There is no new vision at this point, the congregation is serving the by-laws and policy rather than the initial vision of the congregation. The leaders of the church recognize this need and approach the managers about considering some radical new solutions, but the managers cannot see how these new ideas fit into their current system.

An example of this was a congregation in California in which a gifted pastor was able to offer his musical talents and created a contemporary worship service that was held during the Sunday school hour. The managers of the church felt this new service was interfering with the church's potluck dinner that followed the adult Sunday school class, so it had to be canceled. They stopped a worship service that was then connecting with thirty-five people in favor of a potluck that attracted about eight.

You can see how leaders feel stress in this kind of system. The managers expect the leaders to maintain the systems they put in place years ago, without a new vision. Leaders are asked to manage when they are wired to lead. This places them in a difficult situation, and they begin to reduce their engagement with the congregation until they eventually disappear.

This leaves our faithful managers, who are working harder and harder, trying to run a system that has fewer human and financial resources. The church becomes less relevant to its community. The church falls below sustainable levels, yet the managers continue to think that the church will flourish again if they just work harder.

During this stage of the congregation's life, the managers are forced to call a new pastor to the church. They will select a pastor who is also a manager, because they feel that he or she will meet the needs of the people in the church the best. They give little thought to the idea that the church is no longer answering the questions that people in their community are asking. This codifies the decline.

My daughter and son-in-law are both pastors. They were in the Disciples search and call system when a congregation in the Midwest requested an interview. The church provided a profile for their consideration. The congregation stated first and foremost that they wanted to grow, and then it said (and I am not making this up), "We are seeking a pastor who will provide traditional worship experiences, follow our by-laws, and maintain our program." It was the job description of a manager. The congregation was convinced that following the by-laws would lead the congregation to growth.

Now before you get ready to tar and feather the managers in your congregation, let's remember who gave them this power. It was the creative dreamers, relational folks, and leaders who gave them the power, even if they did so reluctantly. We must recognize that managers are deeply motivated people who love God just as much as any of the rest of us. The point of this is not to target this group of Christian as the scapegoats, but rather challenge the managers in our congregations to recognize the need for other gifts in the church and to engage them at the right time in the congregation's life-cycle.

Consider what would happen with a congregation once it starts down the slope of decline if the managers would empower the creative people in their congregation with a visioning process that didn't just tinker with the system. Consider what would happen if relational people were infected with a new compelling vision for the church. Imagine the new gifted people they could bring into the fold. Or think about what would happen if the leaders of a congregation were empowered to launch new enterprises without having their budget disappear or hearing criticism that stops a new initiative.

One Last Thing about Life-cycle

Congregations that are starting to decline can return to vitality by returning to the opposite side of the curve, provided they are still sustainable. If a congregation has just started to decline, it needs to revisit its program life. A congregation that adapts its program can return to a growth cycle.

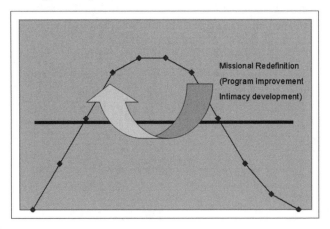

Missional Redefinition
(Program improvement
Intimacy development)

If a congregation has slid to the point that it is losing its relational people, it can return to intimacy development by providing more opportunities in which people can gather together, pray for one another, and rekindle their love for each other.

Once a congregation has slid below sustainable levels, it needs something more dramatic, a separation from the life-cycle that begins to let go of old ways before embracing a new way of being. A helpful paradigm for this has been Theory U.

Theory U was developed by C. Otto Scharmer, a MIT lecturer who developed a concept of leadership theory of how to open our minds, emotions, and wills to moments of discovery and mutual understanding.[4] While Scharmer is an organizational theorist, his paradigm was informed by eastern religious practice. It was not his intention, but Scharmer has identified a Christian process of redemption.

Theory U can be an exciting way to empower people to participate in an ongoing, creative, expanding network of faithful people across a congregation who are open to dreaming, listening, hoping, and making ideas possible.

Scharmer names a process of downloading, suspending, redirecting, sensing, and letting go that allows for allowing something new to come. It can be a spiritual process that first calls a congregation toward having an open mind, open heart, and most importantly an open will.

As a congregation loses its sense of mission, it begins to decline. Even though a congregation is declining, it has human, financial, and facility resources. It is at this point that transformational processes are effective at helping the congregation redefine its mission and to transform into a new way of being.

When a congregation has crossed the line of sustainability, however, it no longer has the resources (human, financial. appropriate facilities) to sustain its ministry without utilizing the resources of a previous generation. At this point the congregation needs to enter into a period of healthy detachment, which leads to cocreating something new. That is why redevelopment leads the congregation to reinvent

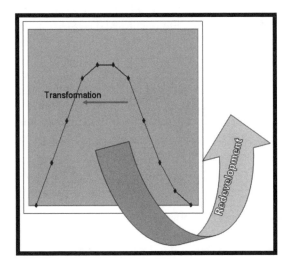

itself, going on in a new direction, rather than returning to a slightly revised mission utilizing the same people, funds, and facilities.

In redevelopment congregations, the leader must work through the act of downloading to a sense of performance that calls participants to leave their organization's downward slope, for a new sense of being. In Scharmer's theory, that means prototyping and embodying a new way of being. This is a spiritual act of redemption that is needed by the pastor while detaching in healthy ways and embracing a new sense of being.

It is predictable that in this time of tremendous change, that is the in-between time of the modern and postmodern world, many more congregations will close unless they can begin to emerge as something new. With the higher costs of operation, we could see a rash of closures in all of our denominations.

Congregations cannot grow or decline without periods of stabilization. I have noted that when a congregation begins, it seems to grow in increments of about thirty people at a time. This is because people in any group need to have time to absorb the new folks. Decline can happen in the same manner. The number of people leaving or disappearing at a time can vary, but it takes a church a while to absorb that loss before it continues its decline.

Decline is much more difficult to measure than growth, because usually people do not leave suddenly, they just quit coming as often. That is why in church development we rely heavily on average worship attendance as a measurement for engagement, rather than membership, which means less and less in the postmodern world.

Finally, let me say that congregational life-cycle is not a predictor that a congregation will die. It also does not predict that a congregation will grow or declines at a steady rate. Congregations are far more complex than that. Life-cycle is important to understand so that congregational leaders gain insight into the development and decline of congregations. Competent church leaders who are passionate about the Gospel can change this trajectory at any time. In addition, conflict, contextual change, and controlling rather than empowering leadership can affect these dynamics quickly.

Size Matters

Congregations act differently depending on their size. Alice Mann of the Alban Institute did some excellent work on congregational size theory.[5] Israel Galindo has also added some depth in his understanding of size dynamics and the "hidden lives of congregations."[6]

The theory is that the size of the church can be an indicator of how that church really functions. While the titles of these categories vary, the concepts are basically the same. Let us take a quick look at churches based on their size.

The Family Size Church

Family size congregations have an average worship attendance of three to fifty on a Sunday morning. These congregations have two to three influential families, and many in the church are related to each other. Each of the families has a "patriarch" or "matriarch" who is the unelected and undisputed leader of the church. These family leaders are very committed members, frequently offering the greatest level of financial support to the church and encouraging their family to do likewise. They have a large investment in the church and make the key decisions for the congregation.

It is not unusual in these congregations for the members to look to the matriarch or patriarch for direction rather than to the pastor. When a congregation takes a vote, you might even see the members looking to the matriarch to see how she votes so they know how to vote. Decisions are not made at the board meeting, they are made by the family leader.

These congregations are fairly closed systems. At a meeting in one of these congregations the matriarch actually said, "We don't want to grow because we wouldn't know these new people." You have to marry into that church to become an authentic part of the congregational system.

Family size congregations want a pastor who will serve as the family chaplain. They will provide pastoral care, Bible study, good sermons (but not too challenging). They are not interested in working with other congregations, but desire to be with each other. They also do not enjoy visits with consultants because of their threat to the congregational system.

Family size congregation can and do make the transition to the next size group. This transition occurs when a congregation has a strong and diplomatic pastor who can achieve buy-in from the matriarch or patriarch. Pastors who try to work around the matriarch or patriarch will soon discover what the word *expendable* means.

The Pastoral Size Church

Galindo uses the term "Shepherding Sized congregation." This congregation averages between 50 and 150 in worship on Sundays.

The members of this kind of congregation get most of their spiritual needs met by a personal relationship with the pastor. The pastor is very relational in this kind of setting.

The pastor is the initiator of programs and usually provides much of the leadership for these congregations. The pastor and the congregation enjoy having a pastor who is in large demand. Much of the change in these congregations comes through the personality of the pastor. The pastor will bring initiatives to the church board, who either approve or disapprove them.

Pastoral size congregations may have some part-time staff members. These churches often hit the 150 ceiling and find it difficult to push through that worship attendance barrier. Malcom Gladwell in his *The Tipping Point* confirms the 150 rule, which states that when more than 150 people are involved, structural matters impede a group's ability to agree on issues and act as one voice.[7] That is to say, congregations that are organized around congregational polity will have much difficulty breaking this barrier.

Most congregations in the United States fall in these first two size categories. According to Kennon Callahan, U.S. congregations average between 3 and 150.[8] A quick look at my denomination indicates that 78 percent of our congregations fit into these categories.

We lift the model of the "relational pastor" as the best kind of pastor, and a lot of us in ministry get seduced by this type of leadership style. It works well for extroverted pastors, but few pastors are actually extroverts. The educational process for clergy rewards introverted personalities, but the parish reality rewards the extroverted personality. Congregations and many clergy have a forced dance around congregational expectations and the pastor's ability to relate that may actually hold a church back from growing.

Congregations that are pastoral size can and do break the 150 barrier, but it is the most difficult barrier for a congregation to break. It requires new attitudes from congregational participants about the role of the pastor, and a pastor who is willing to work in very new ways. It requires leader development and empowerment, as well as a clear congregational sense of identity.

The Program Size Church

Program size congregations have 150 to 300 people in worship on average. This church operates at a more complex level than the previously mentioned sizes. The pastor's role in this kind of a congregation is more of a program manager's role.

Program size congregations have enough resources to employ a staff. That staff delivers pastoral care, small group life, and ministry. The pastor's role is more as the resident theologian. He or she reminds the members of the "why" behind the activities and practices the congregation is engaged in.

The congregation find their spiritual lives formed by their engagement in different church programs and activities. This is in stark contrast to the pastoral size church, where much of their formation comes from the pastor. These participants also learn how to become leaders. Program size churches have opportunities within smaller groups to identify and develop people into leaders, and they do so with great intentionality.

Even fewer congregations push through the 350 barrier to become a corporate church or megachurch.

The Corporate Size Church

Corporate size churches average between 300 and 500 worshipers each Sunday. These represent only about 8 percent of the congregations in the United States and are highly complex. The pastor is more of a CEO than in any other system. He or she rarely has much of a relationship with parishioners, yet this pastor is an important symbol for the congregation's vision and character.

Penny Becker describes this kind of congregation well:

> ...intimacy is less valued here as a public good. Providing members with intimate connections or a feeling of belonging are low priorities...although here too some individuals can find close friends by seeking them out. These congregations are participative, but they are more like branches in a social movement organization, with a strong mission, than are democracies, which have a more diffuse mission.[9]

The corporate size congregation enables individuals to shape their faith through dynamic, high-quality worship. They also offer tremendous options for faith development. Many have a rotation of classes to help new Christians learn the basics of faith in a systematic way. They have the financial and human resources to spin many plates at one time, casting a wide net of service over the community.

The Megachurch

Churches with more than 500 in worship are rare. Only 1 percent of all congregations become this large, yet they serve about 25 percent of all church participants in America.[10]

There is some evidence that as the Boomer population ages, megachurches will likely have to adapt again to meet the needs of new generations. People in their twenties are very intentional about finding authentic relationships, especially when it comes to their spiritual life. As you will see later, Boomers and the Silent Generation were attracted to the very large church system. This trend is already starting to change, yet it is too early to tell. Megachurches have an excellent track record when it comes to adapting to culture.

Tipping Points and Change

The first church I served as a pastor in Idaho had had an average worship attendance of sixty people for the last twenty years. The church had no Sunday school or youth program, and was aging more and more each year. Shortly after I began, a young woman with six children started attending our church. Within three years the church had doubled in size, had a growing ministry with children, and a youth program that was the envy of other congregations in the community.

I give a lot of credit to that one family. Those six children and their regular attendance at the church helped the church achieve a tipping point. Before long, these children were bringing their friends to church, and soon the children who had been in the wings of the church started coming more regularly. It became fashionable to be a part of the youth group.

Just 20 Percent of the Congregation Can Tip the System

It takes very few people to change a situation. Malcom Gladwell lifts up the 80/20 Principle in *Tipping Point.* Economists and epidemiologists have known about this principle for years. A tiny group of people can lead to some extraordinary changes in a community. The great anthropologist Margaret Mead understood this dynamic as well when she said: " Never doubt that a small group of thoughtful, committed, citizens can change the world. Indeed, it is the only thing that ever has."

The 80/20 Principle basically states that 80 percent of the work will be accomplished by 20 percent of the people. Sociologists will say that just 20 percent of all criminals commit 80 percent of all crime. Insurance actuaries will claim that just 20 percent of motorists cause 80 percent of accidents. Social workers will tell you that 20 percent of beer drinkers drink 80 percent of the beer.[11]

Church development people have long understood this principle. I'm not even sure where I first read about the 80/20 Principle in church life. We know that in most congregations, 20 percent of the congregation do 80 percent of the work and give 80 percent of the congregation's income. The other 80 percent of the congregation provide 20 percent.

For some reason, however, congregations feel it is important to appease 100 percent of the congregation when it comes to change. A vital congregation would never distinguish the "doers" from the "cruisers"; a vital congregation does not let the "tyranny of a few" control the church's future.

Congregations hate conflict and will avoid it at most costs. This avoidance keeps congregations from making important decisions about their future, since a single "no" vote would signal the possibility of conflict.

Gil Rendle, a church development expert, sheds some light on that dynamic. He points out that every organization has key positional people. He states that 2 percent of the population will be against any new initiative, and that another 10 percent will lean heavily against any new initiative. He also points out that 2 percent of the population will vote in favor of any new initiative and another 10 percent will lean in favor of any new thing. That means that only 76 percent of any group can be helpful in making a decision about a church's future. His point is that few congregations will ever achieve 100 percent consensus on any change, unless the church is pretty small. Churches tend to hold out for 100 percent consensus, which is simply not likely.[12]

It only takes a few people to change a congregation, but it takes the right people. It requires that people are willing to be counted and that they have an affinity toward action. It doesn't hurt if the congregation respects these people. Just a few people who have passion and a clear vision for a future, who can talk with enthusiasm, can turn a boat that has been on a straight course for a very long time.

Gladwell offers numerous examples of how small groups of people can turn entire communities around. My favorite example is his story regarding the resurgence in sales of Hush Puppies® shoes.[13]

Hush Puppies was a popular shoe brand between the 1960s and the 1980s. The brand was losing ground as American style sense was changing. In 1995 the brand only sold 30,000 pairs. But in 1996, the brand sold 450,000 pairs. What changed was that a few trendsetting individuals in the East Village and Soho of New York began wearing them to make a fashion statement that they were not like everyone else. Before long, Hush Puppies were being sold in secondhand clothing shops because they were difficult to purchase at major shoe chains. Soon more and more "trendsetters" were wearing the shoes, and sales exploded.

The same can happen in a congregation. A few people who show some enthusiasm for a new way of being can change the entire course of a congregation. It doesn't take everyone in a unanimous vote.

Designed to Say No–Tipping to Say Yes

Rendle uses the 80/20 Principle to bolster the next point. Congregations are designed to say "no." The purpose of by-laws and orderly processes such as "rules of order" is to make change difficult.

Dick Hamm, the former General Minister of the Christian Church (Disciples of Christ) and a church development expert says it best: "We bring a resolution to the floor of the Assembly, argue about it for the allotted twelve minutes, and then somehow expect that the Holy Spirit has been present enough that we can begin to guess the will of God based on that limited conversation and vote."[14]

Rendle points out that true discernment about a church's mission can only come through prayer, reflection, and episodic conversations. That means more than twelve minutes and more than one conversation on the same conditional topic. At the end of the day, however, a church does have to make a decision. The failure of a congregation to make a decision about its future is in and of itself a decision. Congregations often are happy with the conversation, just not making a commitment. That makes the ministry of a congregation difficult to deliver.

I used to work with a social worker who was committed to working with the mentally ill in our community. He was the kind of guy who liked to keep all his options open until the very last second. I like to keep my options open too, but I have a calendar with lots of appointments that I have to honor. I remember one time we had to make a hiring decision that would impact our organization's future. I was trying to line up candidates and to get the social worker to commit to a date so we could work together in making this decision. It was a frustrating conversation in which he could not commit to a hour-long meeting at any time. It wasn't that he had obligations; he was just trying to keep his schedule open. We eventually held the interviews without him.

Congregations who cannot make a commitment toward ministry are equally frustrating. We feel that if we just take more time, keep our options open, or maybe hold our tongue, the situation will change without the congregation going through the painful process of making a decision. That is why congregations write fairly meaningless mission statements: "We want to be the church of Jesus Christ for everybody." We write these statements with good intentions, but we are writing to get approval by everyone. Fruitful conversation will enable people the space and time to have a conversation. But it will also have a time of decision where people bring their insights to the table and in prayer decide what future God is calling them toward.

A coworker and I worked with a congregation in Washington State that had a great history in a small agricultural town. The members had been active in Disciples regional activities, and the church had a lovely facility. However, they were struggling with sustainability .

The community around the congregation had changed dramatic-ally. This once largely Anglo community was now 82 percent Hispanic. The crops in that area had changed for some reason, requiring a great deal more labor, which led to a large infusion of Hispanic workers. Spanish-speaking people now owned many businesses in the community and there were signs everywhere in Spanish.

It was clear to people who had worked with the congregation in the past that this church could expand its witness to the growing Hispanic community in their midst. Numerous denominational leaders had suggested they consider this, but the congregation would not make a decision.

In our process, we also suggested that they consider some method of redevelopment that would include the Spanish-speaking population. We then gave them a plan for breaking up the congregation into small groups, with trained leaders guiding the members in a series of conversations about the condition of their church and community. At the end of six weeks, we asked them to see if there was consensus from the groups.

To our surprise the congregation made a decision and are currently seeking a Hispanic pastor to help morph them to serve the growing community in the near future. This congregation's members, and those who had worked with them, knew this was a scenario that the congregation could achieve, but the congregation would never have the conversation, let alone bring the conversation to a conclusion. We were surprised, because in twenty years the congregation never had the conversation, and then in just six weeks they made a decision.

Generational Tipping Points

For the first time in history, churches are trying to serve six different generations at one time. People are living longer, and culture is changing rapidly. This means that the chasms between the different worldviews of a teen and someone in her forties and with someone in his eighties are wide. A church is challenged to bring growth opportunities for all generational groups, yet these groups know little about each other.

If a congregation is heavily loaded with older generations, it will likely have difficulty making changes that are needed to be more inclusive of all age groups. Congregations reach a tipping point when they have at least a 50-50 split between the Boomers and older group and the group that is younger.

As mentioned earlier, older adults are striving for stabilization in their lives. They want their churches to remain stable, with few changes, so that the church will be there to bury them when life ends. Younger participants are seeking ways that the church can adapt to its current context. For a congregation to consider change, it must have representation from people who are not seeking stabilization as a part of the decision-making process.

Tipping Tenure Rates

It will be difficult for congregations to consider change if the vast majority of the congregation has been involved with the church five years or more. It takes new people in the system in order for a congregation to make new decisions, regardless of the age of participants.

I worked with a congregation in Canada that had a good spread of participants from many generations, but everyone had been born into that congregation. Only 10 percent of the congregation had joined in the past five years. Most of the people had been a part of that church for generations. You can imagine how new initiatives would be met in that circumstance.

New people bring new experiences, new ideas, and new energy to a church's system. Without them in decision–making positions, the church misses a great opportunity to grow. It is difficult to for folks that are "used to each other." to empower newcomers.

The tipping point for tenure rates appears to be around five years. Vital congregations will have a 50-50 ratio of those who have participated five years or more compared with those who have participated less than five years.

Behavioral Tipping Points

Percept, a company that provides demographic services for a number of denominations, has developed a tool called the iChange® indicator.[15] This is a little questionnaire that can be taken by congregational members to measure an individual's emotional response to change as well as his or her behavioral response once the person is confronted with change.

We have used this indicator with about eighty congregational groups, and we are starting to observe some tipping points.

Emotional response is how react once they are confronted with a need for change. As you can imagine, there are a wide range of emotions here. People are either excited or energized by the thought of change, or they are immediately fearful and start to panic. Other people just cope with it.

To tip the system of a congregation, you will need at least 20 to 33 percent of the participants to be energized or excited about a change. If more than 33 percent of the congregation are fearful or in a panic about change, it is not likely that the system will entertain the notion of having conversations about change.

While that information is helpful in finding a tipping point for conversations about change, the behavioral response to change is crucial. This is the measurement of how many people in a church will actually do something when confronted with change.

Some people are actually wired to be reactive and resistant to any kind of change. They will go to great lengths to sabotage changes that are suggested in the church parking lot or on the telephone. Other people are proactive. Still other people are fairly passive.

The tipping point for congregations is when 20 to 33 percent of the participants are proactive toward change. That is to say, they will do what is needed to enact the kind of changes the group desires. If congregations have too large a number of participants that have resistant behavior, or too large a group that is passive, change will not likely occur.

You really have to consider both categories to see if your church is potentially at a tipping point. For example, we worked with a congregation in the Midwest in which 45 percent of the congregation were energized when discussing change. However, when it came time to enact the change, only one person had proactive behavior. The rest of the leaders of that congregation were either passive or resistant. The congregation loved to talk about change, but few people did anything to change the situation.

Talking about Conditions

An issue that keeps congregations from making deliberate decisions about their future is their inability to simply name conditions instead of getting into problem-solving methods. Committees are designed to solve problems. They follow the familiar, linear pattern of identifying the problem, suggesting solutions, and making a decision that leads to implementation and returns the church to the status quo. This method works great if you are trying to return to something that needs to be the same as before. However, if a church has been declining for a long period of time, this kind of method is only going to accelerate decline.

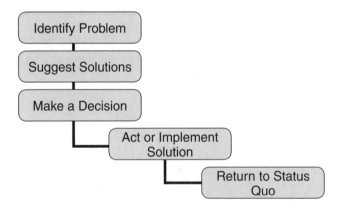

My friend and colleague Lori Adams has a great example of how this method works. A few years ago she was faced with having to replace her furnace. She had an older home, built in the 1930s, and the upstairs was always cold in the winter. She asked the furnace man who was giving a bid if they could put a larger unit in this time so that her upstairs would be warmer. The man patiently explained that the reason her upstairs was cold was because the house did not have a cold-air return. She could pump more heat into the system, but the system was flawed, so the result would have been more cold winters no matter how much heat was put in. Complex systems like congregations cannot be "fixed" by a problem-solving method. Identifying the problem is not enough. At one congregation we almost worked with, in a church meeting, the congregation was discussing the opportunity to have a consultation process. They were discussing their declining situation and that the church was just barely sustainable in its current condition. The turning point in that conversation was when a respected elder of the congregation stood up and said: "We know what the problem is. We do not have enough people in our church. All we need to do is get more people, and our problem is solved." The congregation voted to not enter into a consultation because they had identified the problem.

Problem-solving does not lead a congregation to adaptive change. The issue for the above congregation was really not the lack of people in the pews, but the way in which the congregation was trying to relate to its context. They will not likely learn this lesson without significant conversation with one another about what is happening in their surrounding area, how it is changing, what the people are like, and what their church could do to make a difference in their lives.

Gil Rendle suggests what he calls "non-synoptic" planning, a series of frequent conversations that list options, but do not come to a conclusion for a period of time. Instead of a twelve-minute

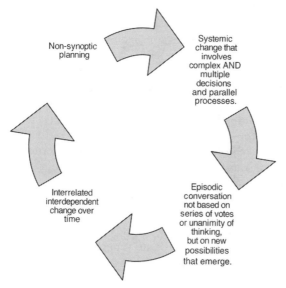

conversation, he recommends conversations that allow the participants to come to similar conclusions about the church's condition based on common measurable facts. This leads to adaptive change, that is, change that enables the congregation to adapt to its environment and meet the needs of those around them.

I was watching an interesting documentary on people who live in Tibet. I wouldn't last very long in these very high altitudes. Yet the Tibetans have adapted to their environment and thrive there. Part of the reason is that they drink lots of yak milk. They drink it every afternoon in a special tea that they brew. This drink is not something that looks particularly appetizing to me. However, yak milk contains 7 percent fat, not the 4 percent we find in cow milk. This higher fat content has allowed the Tibetans to adapt to the cold winters and high altitude.

When you think about it, the Tibetan people didn't have a blue ribbon task force that studied the lack of fat in their diets. They didn't make a list of potential sources of fat and then decide on yak milk, which they voted on the next month.

They likely began by someone experimenting, talking about it, trying it with tea, watching those who drank it, and eventually acquiring a taste for it. Someone likely said, "lets try it with tea." Then eventually they noticed that the guy who didn't drink yak tea was always cold and getting very skinny. "This tea must be good for us," someone must have said sometime. That is the difference between problem-solving and adaptive change.

(But can you imagine the poor fellow that had to milk a yak for the first time? That had to take courage.)

Congregations that are invested in conversations about their conditions are also willing at some point to attempt some new things, which leads the congregation to adapting. This does not mean there will not be failures in the congregation's life. In the mid-1970s an educational theorist named John Holt wrote a provocative book entitled *How Children Fail.* Holt suggested that the educational process was punishing kids for their failing rather than encouraging children to try things beyond their reach.[16]

My children benefited from his writings. I remember my children were always given "bonus words" on their spelling tests. These were large words that children their age would hardly ever use. If they could spell them right, they earned bonus points; if they got them wrong, they lost nothing. The process allowed children to see that trying something could bring benefit, and not cost you anything.

At the same time, I watched their grandparents struggle with learning computers. My parents were scared to use an ATM cash machine until well after the year 2000. They just knew if they did something wrong, the machine would take their card, and they wouldn't be allowed to use the machine again. They were also slow to try computers. They believed the machines were too fast and they were not sure they could trust the computer's math. My children, on the other hand, are willing to try to get the computer to do anything. They edit photos, store music, download movies, and much more. They can make a computer dance because they know there is no permanent punishment for making a mistake. You can always reboot.

Wouldn't it be great if congregations felt that same permission? New congregations have nothing to lose by being innovative. It is very inspiring to be part of a congregation that knows what they are called to do and is willing to try a number of different methods to succeed. Vital congregations are willing to run things up the flagpole, and if nobody salutes, they bring it down fast, with nothing lost.

Is Your Church Vulnerable to Knuckleheads?

While it is important to see the dynamics and possible tipping points your church may be experiencing, it is also important to ask, "is our church vulnerable to knuckleheads?" Congregations that have long tenure rates, older generational groups, long histories of decline, and poor finances will often enter into periods of vulnerability. This is particularly true if the congregation had the leadership of a patriarch or matriarch who has taken ill or died.

A knucklehead is someone who leads the congregation toward initiatives that lead to either a capital reduction of church assets or a major shift in the congregation's core values that dishonors the witness of the congregation's past.

I have witnessed at least six congregations who have been the victims of embezzlement from individuals whom the congregation has trusted. I have seen congregations sell beautiful facilities to develop a fund that provides for the long-term salary needs of a pastor who serves only a very small group.

These are some of the indicators that a congregation may be vulnerable:

1. Lack of participation by congregational officers at board meetings
2. Lack of oversight of congregation's finances with little reporting to the board

3. Aging congregation where individuals are getting desperate to see the witness continue and will do anything to see it happen
4. Willingness of the congregation to give up power to any new person regardless of the person's commitment or understanding of the congregation's values and beliefs
5. High distrust of the congregation for denominational structures and leaders
6. Inability of the congregation to pay their bills
7. Small numbers of participants with any personal energy
8. Lack of members with personal success with financial matters or even organizational work

Now let us look at a couple of examples. A congregation once sold their church building to create a new ministry. They received $2 million from a developer and immediately invested the funds in the stock market with a knucklehead who was new to the congregation who happened to be an investment counselor. Denominational leaders tried to encourage the congregation to invest with one of the denomination's financial units because of their oversight and good experience, not to mention their ethical investment standards. But the knucklehead convinced the congregation that he could earn more in the free market. This was at the end of the 1990s, right before the dot-com bust. The congregation almost immediately lost $500,000 of their investment and has yet to recover their loss with their current portfolio. Meanwhile, the knucklehead earned his stock commission.

Another congregation was down to just twenty members. None of the participants had personal financial success. At a meeting that I conducted with individuals of the church, a new couple attended. This couple had been very active in their former congregation and seemed very attractive and hopeful to the congregational members who were burned out. Within moments of establishing themselves with the group, they mentioned that they knew an unemployed pastor from their former congregation who could help lead Bible studies and even provide excellent leadership for the church, although the church already had a faithful part-time pastor.

I was alarmed at that meeting when none of the members asked about this pastor, why he left the former congregation, or if he knew anything about this congregation's values or beliefs. Instead, they were willing to sign the guy up on the spot. I had no idea if this pastor friend were a knucklehead, but the congregation certainly displayed its vulnerability.

I also worked with another Midwestern congregation that could not produce financial records. They had not had a financial report by the financial secretary for the past six years. Her comment to the church board when they asked for a report was "Either you trust me or you don't." She basically told them she would not give them a report. The fact that the congregation didn't push her indicates vulnerability. Although I doubted the woman was embezzling funds, I was suspicious of her power needs and how she was using the church finances to control the church by ensuring she was the only person who knew about their financial conditions. She made sure people would ask her permission for any spending in the church.

The above scenarios may seem so obvious you cannot picture your church falling into such circumstances, but they happen all the time, particularly in churches not willing to look at their situation honestly. It is my hope that by sharing this book you will have a common vocabulary for discussing the conditions of your church, and where it is today in its life-cycle. I also hope that you can tell whether your church is sustainable at its level, and can begin to tell if your church is open toward considering change.

Questions for Discussion

1. Does our congregation have a clear sense of our mission, and are we united toward accomplishing it?
2. Does our congregation have balanced resources (volunteers, leaders, facilities and finances)? In what area do we need more resources?
3. Where would you say our congregation is in relationship to the life-cycle graph?
4. Of the types of people who "drive the bus" at different times in a congregation's life-cycle, who would you say is driving ours today? (Creative People, Relational Folks, Leaders, or Managers)
5. Which of the size categories best describes our congregation?
6. Does our congregation engage in episodic conversations (non-synoptic planning) or are we locked into the "problem-solving method"?
7. Does our church show any of the danger signs that we might be vulnerable to knuckleheads?

4

Good to Great Congregations

Churches can learn and apply lessons from other organizations, as long as they keep in mind how they are different from those organizations. In 2001 Jim Collins wrote a best seller entitled *Good to Great*.[1] He described his landmark research with businesses that had outperformed competing companies in the marketplace. He wanted to know what it would take for a good company to become a great one. He found some significant differences in the way in which great companies do business and identified the common threads of their success.

As he continued his consulting work with other businesses, he discovered he was being asked by more and more organizations to discuss his findings. This led him to write the companion booklet, *Good to Great and the Social Sectors: Why Business Thinking Is Not the Answer*.[2]

At Church Extension, we have used this paradigm to aid us in our organizational development. It has been exciting to watch how we continue to struggle with understanding our "deep center" (a concept defined later in this chapter). Lori Adams, one of the codevelopers of the New Beginnings© Service that I work with, is deeply immersed in Church Extension's organizational development. She suggested that we add this paradigm in our work with New Beginnings congregations. At this writing we have worked with more than 150 congregations through this service, and I can attest to how this paradigm enables congregations to move from being *good* congregations to *great* congregations.

I recommend Collins's books. They are loaded ideas you can apply to your congregation related to leadership, recruitment of volunteers, disciplined people, approaches, thought, and action.

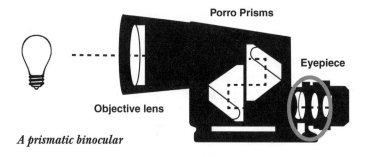

Porro Prisms

Eyepiece

Objective lens

A prismatic binocular

The part I would like to discuss is how our congregations can begin to use additional lenses in our binoculars to begin focusing on future ministry. These lenses help to bring clarity to an image we might be viewing and are called the eyepiece. These three lenses are great ways to look at your church so that you can begin to imagine your future ministry.

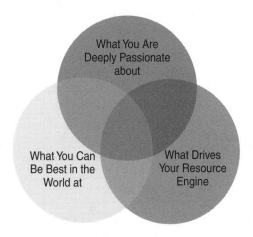

What You Are Deeply Passionate about

What You Can Be Best in the World at

What Drives Your Resource Engine

Passion

Passion is where we find our energy. Our passion is the ministry that we care a great deal about. We have mentioned the life-cycle of a congregation and how this element is essential for congregations at the start of their life-cycle. We have also mentioned how congregations that lose sight of that passion are not usually on the growth side of the life-cycle. The more we think about our passion for ministry, the more clarity we get for focusing our vision.

Passion is the energy within us that enables us to persevere. The more strongly we feel about something, the more likely we are to achieve it. As in the urban legend of a mother who lifts a car off of her baby, when we are passionate about something, we find a way to make things happen.

Measuring the passion of a congregation is difficult. It is important, however, that congregational leaders face the brutal reality: "Is our congregation motivating people to live life more abundantly, as Jesus calls us to, or are we just going through the motions?"

I suggest two subjective ways to measure a congregation's passion. The first is worship. Regardless of the style of worship, you can tell people who are passionate about their faith as opposed to those who are enduring worship so they can see their friends afterwards. It is evident in the music, prayers, and even in the announcements. Do you see energy in those elements?

Another subjective way to measure energy and passion is how people talk about their church. Are they energized when discussing their engagement with the church? When you ask a group about points of commitment with the church, do they light up, or do they speak about their ministries as a duty?

There also are two more objective ways to get a hint about the congregation's energy and passion. Generational data and tenure rates can give you an idea about where a congregation might be at this stage in its development.

Generational Data

When you count people in your church by their generation, does your congregation match the demographics of your community? When we do a New Beginnings© assessment, we count regular participants and their ages and then match them to the community. This produces a graph like the sample below:

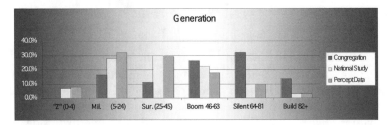

The dark grey bars on this graph indicate the number of congregational participants in each of these generational categories. The light gray bars show the Percept data for the same community, in contrast with the national averages (white bars).

You can see that this sample congregation is much older on average than the community. It also shows that 79 percent of this congregation is more than forty-six years of age. No one in this congregation is younger than four, and though there are a few participants between the ages of five and twenty-four, they are practically all children being raised by grandparents.

Bill Easum maintains that no more of than 50 percent\% of vital congregations are older than the age of fifty.[3] This is because young people bring passion and energy, new creative ideas, and expertise in using new technologies.

The life issue for many older adults is to head for stabilization. That is to say, when you get in your fifties you have a different mindset. You are starting to think about retirement, about a routine for your daily life, about cementing your support network around you.

The life issues for younger adults are different. They are building their lives. They are willing to take a chance on something new. They abhor routine, and they want to use their time in a way that makes a difference.

While a congregation may have good generational participation, it is important to measure whether all ages are engaged in leadership. It does little good to have a good generational mix if the congregation is not taking advantage of what younger individuals can bring to the table. It is the tension between those who are seeking stabilization and those who are building their lives that brings dynamic decisions for the future of a church.

Tenure Rates

The longer someone has been a part of a congregation, the more they act like someone interested primarily in stability. That is why it is also important to measure tenure rates. The tenure rate of a participant is the period of time in which a person has been participating with a congregation. It has nothing to do with membership.

While we honor and respect long tenured participants, it is important to have new people who can bring new perspectives and ideas to a congregation. We measure these rates in our New Beginning assessment as well.

This chart represents a sample congregation in which 79 percent of the participants have been in this church for five years or longer. This is a congregation that is built around stabilization; they get visitors, but few remain.

Again Easum suggests that a vital congregation would have a 50-50 split of those attending five years or longer with those who have attended less than five years. It does little good to have new participants in a congregation however, unless the church can engage them at the table of decision-making.[4]

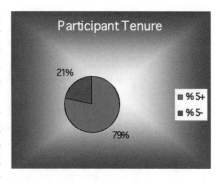

Generally speaking, congregations that are loaded with long-term members who are seeking stabilization will not have the energy of congregations with good generational and tenure mixes. However, as with all stereotypes, these statistics do not hold true for all people. Spirit-led individuals who have been in a church for more than five years or who are older than fifty can defy the conventional wisdom, especially once they're aware of their possible propensity to pursue stability.

You know a passionate congregation when you see it. It is filled with people who have been moved by God and who have a deep desire to be disciples that stay close to Christ, listening to his words and seeking to be instruments of his peace.

What You Can Be Best in the World at

It seems a little bold to think that your congregation can be the best in the world at anything, but that possibility does exist. No single congregation can save the world, but it can be the best in the world at something.

The last parish I served in Seattle was the best at working with gifted children in our community. This group of very intelligent and active young people is often overlooked. People think, "They will be OK" and focus their energies on other youth and children's issues. Yet this group has some special needs that cannot be dealt with in normal ways. It took us nearly ten years to discover what we could be best at, but once we did, and made it our focus, we had a special niche that no other congregation could excel at.

While only 1 to 2 percent of the community's children were considered "gifted," these children composed 45 percent of our program's attendees. The rest of the kids were pretty bright as well. This meant we needed to write our own church school curriculum and provide educational experiences that encouraged their creative juices. The youth group was able to perform musicals that they had written themselves and to take their music on the road. They did the choreography and pretty much self-directed their plays.

This did not mean that we ignored "normal" kids; all of the children were engaged in a dynamic, challenging program. It just meant that we took seriously what we could be best at and worked hard to empower a specific group of people. The whole church benefited as a result. Older participants loved the energy and enthusiasm, as well as the creativity, of this group. It gained the church notability in the community. And people wanted for their children to be involved in a church like that.

The congregation made a large difference in those people's lives. For a period of their lives a church was open to them and gave them an experience they will never forget. Because of it, they know that God loves them unconditionally. It is painful to me that some are not involved in congregations today because they have not found a church that would empower their gifts that they would love to share.

Chances are your congregation is already best at something, and you have yet to articulate what that might be. Frederick Buechner says, "Our vocation is the intersection between our greatest passion and the world's greatest need."[5] A "best at" congregation has to focus on its community. It does no good to have the greatest children's program in the world if you live in a gated "adults only" community.

It also does little good to be "best at" something that people are not passionate about. A congregation we worked with a couple of years ago was filled with teachers and social workers and was in the middle of a community of people who had little education, many without even a high school diploma. We suggested that they consider using their gifts toward creating a GED program, but the church participants wisely said: "Yes, we could do that, but I can't get excited about doing it." They recognized that their passion did not relate to that need.

The best ways to measure a congregation's "best at" is to look at both the congregation and the community and begin to identify ways in which the church is relevant to its setting. One way this can be done is to exegete your community as you would the scriptures. Look at the demographic data using some of the methods described in chapter 2. Ask yourself: "What are the needs in this community just screaming for attention?"

But you also need to look at your congregation. When are the people in our church most passionate? What are they doing? When they talk to others about the church, what are they saying? Somewhere in this intersection of passion and community need is what your congregation can be best at in the world.

What Drives Your Resource Engine

The third lens that Collins suggests looking at is your congregation's resource engine. Collins states how this circle is different from business:

> The question is not "how much money do we make?" but "How can we develop a sustainable resource engine to deliver superior performance relative to our mission?"[6]

Remember, when we consider resources, we think about four legs: Volunteers, Leaders, Facilities, and Finances. These four legs must be equally strong to support a ministry fully. Congregations that do not have the financial resources for their ministry are constantly skimping on its quality. A congregation full of volunteers, but with no leaders, are not able to deliver sustainable ministry. A church facility that eats up the congregation's financial resources while not supporting the ministry of the congregation taxes both the volunteer and financial resources that could be used to sustain ministry.

Volunteers

What is your sense about the volunteer capacity of your congregation? Do you have problems recruiting people for tasks? Do you spend too much of volunteers' time in the decision-making process rather than the direct delivery of ministry?[7]

Score yourself on a scale of one to ten, with "ten" "We have a large pool of volunteers eager to deliver ministry services." A "one" would mean "We can't get anyone to volunteer for anything."

Leadership

Leaders are defined as people who can motivate others to go somewhere they would not have gone voluntarily without their leadership. They are not a majority of the population, and they are a golden resource for a congregation. They have creativity and the ability to engage people in conversations about a better future.

Make a list of leaders in your congregation. Are you using their gifts or are you filling vacancies on the church board? Is there a system for identifying, nurturing, and empowering leaders? Score your church with a "ten" meaning "We have abundant leaders waiting in the wings." A "one" would mean "We do not have any leaders, including the people currently serving in our leadership positions."

Facilities

Facilities must be the right size for the mission of a congregation. This is a little easier to measure. First of all, do you have enough space, or too much? To measure this use the formula below:

(Average Worship Attendance X 80) / Total Sq. Feet
= Percentage of Space needed

Generally speaking, a congregation will need to use between 60 and 80 percent of their facility's space. If the percentage is below 60 it is an indicator that the church facility is too large for the group of people trying to maintain it.

Another measurement to consider is what percentage of the church budget goes to the operation of the facility and what percentage to the total operating fund. The following formula will get that answer for you:

(Sum of All Facility Operating Expenses)
/ Total Operating Expenses

If that percentage exceeds 25 percent, it means that the congregation is skimping ministry and taxing volunteers to maintain a facility that is too large.

Finally, some additional questions to consider are: Is the building maintained well, or are there numerous deferred maintenance items? Do our church participants live near us, or are they driving in from some other part of the community? Is our space appropriate for the kind of ministry we are trying to deliver? Are we located in a place where people can find us?

Score your church with a "ten" meaning "Our building is just the right size and in the right place with no problems." A "one" would mean "Our building is too large/small and is not accessible to those who would benefit from our ministry services."

Finances

This category has three areas of measurement: income sources, expense percentages, and assets and investments.

You can measure these items using the formulas in the ministry plan section. The question you are exploring is, "Do we have the financial capacity needed to sustain our ministry?"

Score your congregation with a "ten" meaning "We have accessible finances in our treasury to fund current and future ministries." A "one" would mean "We are not sure how we are going to pay the bills this week."

Now take your scores from each resource area. If these were table leg lengths, would your table wobble? Would the table be high enough to sit at, or is your church like a giant sitting at a kindergartner's desk?

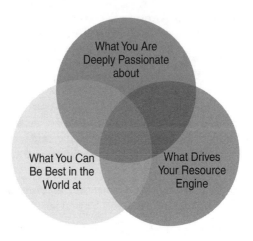

Putting It Together

Consider the three components we have just discussed. If you think of them as overlapping circles, as in the diagram above, what Collins calls a "deep center" begins to emerge where all three circle merge. The deep center for a congregation is where its passion, "best at," and resource engine merge. That is where the church is functioning at its best.

What Collins discovered in his research applies to us today. The congregations that excel have discovered their deep center. They are the best at a specific ministry, their people are passionate about doing it, and they have ample resources to keep the ministry sustainable. Most congregations have not yet discovered this deep center. Many have even quit looking. At the dawn of this postmodern world, congregations must find their deep centers if they hope to sustain ministry.

Strategies for Congregational Development

You may recall the movie *My Big Fat Greek Wedding.* The Greek father of this first-generation immigrant family had one cure for everything...spray Windex® on it. If your wrist hurt, he would spray you; if you had a headache, he would spray your head. It was ridiculously funny. The point is that there is no single approach any congregation can use for its development. I would like to suggest three types of strategies that are appropriate for congregations at different points of their life-cycle.

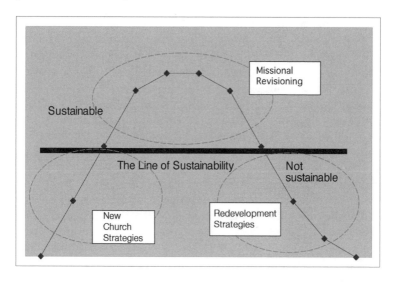

New Church Strategies

One of the ten top reasons that new churches fail is they try to borrow another church's vision for ministry. As Jim Griffith says in his recent book, someone attends a seminar at some megachurch and returns home to replicate that kind of church in their community.[8]

Church planting is so difficult because it is not something you can replicate at will. It has to be the right kind of church in the right place at the right time. A new congregation requires just as much ministry planning as an existing congregation. The issue for these congregations is often that their resource engine is hardly running in the initial stages of a congregation's life. But they make up for this deficit with passion and a vision about what they can be "best in the world at."

Missional Revisioning

Congregations at the top of the life-cycle are usually sustainable. They have resources, but their passion may be starting to wane. They are faithful about their ministry, but for some reason the church is not in sync with its context. These are congregations that are ripe for missional revisioning.

Most businesses revisit their mission every three years to see if they are hitting a community's sweet spot. Most major corporations change their logo and tag lines every twenty or thirty years. Coke® changes their labeling even more frequently. They know that their "brand" takes time to get noticed. They also know that an old brand will make the company appear dated and irrelevant.

A congregation we worked with in Arizona was developed in the 1950s with a mission to serve the needs of farm workers in their small community. Because it was an isolated town, they needed to provide public health care and a nursery for small children. Now, nearly sixty years later, the congregation is in the middle of an exploding suburban community that has a new retail core and vital health services. The needs for which it was originally formed no longer exist. The farms are gone, and a whole new type of person lives in the area. This church is in the process of revisioning their ministry. They know they cannot continue to do their ministry the same way.

The term may not be totally accurate for all congregations at this point in their life-cycle. Revisioning implies that the congregation had a vision, which is not always the case. Many churches were formed because of a "franchise mentality." That is to say, we (a denomination) build a church somewhere because we don't have one there. They were modeled after the mother church with little thought about the peculiarities of that area. For these congregations, the strategy of developing a vision for a ministry is imperative.

Revisioning congregations can grow and develop new ministries that allow the church to adapt to the needs of people in their changing culture and context.

Redevelopment Strategies

Congregations that have slid down the slope and are struggling with sustainability need another kind of strategy. Simply claiming a new vision for ministry will not be enough for that kind of congregation. It may simply need something more radical. Congregations that are struggling with sustainability need to address more than two aspects of Collins's diagram. They may be lacking passion or program or resources to have the church resemble any level of vitality. These congregations may not have the leadership or volunteers necessary for developing a vital ministry. They may have tremendous demographic differences with the community, such as age, or worse yet, they may not have relevance to their context because almost everyone lives outside of the community.

There are five basic strategies for redevelopment, with hybrids for each strategy.

Morphing

Morphing is best applied to a congregation that has large differences with its context. This would usually be a congregation in an area where the racial ethnic make-up has changed. It can also work in a congregation whose members have aged while the community is still quite young.

Morphing changes the target for ministry to a new group. This occurs by calling a new pastor who represents the affinity group the church realizes it must reach. The congregation then changes its composition with time, passing on leadership to new participants.

Relocating

Sometimes a congregation could be the right people in the wrong part of the community. This would be a congregation that has good human and financial resources, but few people from the context in which the church building is located.

A congregation we did a pilot study with was located in Texas. This church was in the oldest part of town, which had become home to mostly low-income, nontraditional families. This was in contrast to a congregation of mostly high-income professionals with traditional families. Over the years the congregation had employed no fewer than three consultants to help the congregation with its visioning process. Each time the consultants recommended the church relocate to the growing part of the community. Each time the congregation rejected the notion and remained in their old facility, which was built in the 1930s.

Today, the growing edge of the community is bustling with development and new housing. The churches in that part of the community are thriving and growing as well. By the time we did our pilot study, the best we could recommend was that they seriously consider closure, which the church reluctantly did. This could have been avoided if the congregation had acted while it still had the resources to relocate.

Another pilot study church in New Orleans did relocate, which enabled them to "right size." This thirty-year-old congregation had a facility that was way too large and had fallen into disrepair. The church had endured a painful split several years earlier, and former members who were bitter spread some nasty rumors about the church throughout the community, so the church had negative appeal in the community.

The sanctuary seated 300, but now only sixty people worshiped there, so you can see the scale of their capacity issues. They were able to trade facilities with a Lutheran congregation that had need for their space. They were able to receive a well-constructed Lutheran building, plus some cash for the excess space. This enabled the congregation a chance to start fresh with a new name.

Today the congregation has a full-time pastor and a growing worship attendance despite Hurricane Katrina. The church has been a leader in providing space for work crews traveling on mission trips to rebuild New Orleans.

Parallel Start

A parallel start is a strategy that can be used when a congregation is aging, but is not a congregation you want to close, because it provides good ministry for people in their old age. These kinds of congregations generally have good facilities, some resources, but not the human capital to build a congregation around because of their being very different from their community.

The congregation allows an outside group to select a new church planter to be their next pastor. This planter will give the congregation 25 percent of his or her time, and provide nurture and care for the church as they begin a new congregation with the other 75 percent of the time.

The new church becomes the priority for that congregation, and the planter has two years to get it established to a level of at least sixty in worship. At the end of that two-year period, the faithful remnant group has an opportunity to melt into the new church, continue their group, or formally close their ministry.

We did this in Portland, Oregon, where we had a congregation of mostly seniors. The church building was large, and things were out of control. The former pastor had just died after a long period of illness. The congregation was down to eleven people in a 30,000 square-foot facility. They had few resources, so they rented the building out to anyone so they could raise money.

Unfortunately, the treasurer had Alzheimer's disease and did not collect rent, nor pay the bills. The utilities were frequently cut off. So many groups had keys to the building that there were constant scheduling problems. Everyone had a rummage sale going, and consequently the building was packed with rummage and old couches everyone knew "someone" would buy.

By establishing an excellent planter in that situation, we were able to use the large facility to start two new congregations while providing care for the senior members of the faithful remnant group. By the end of two years, none of the faithful remnant was alive, and while their church closed, their witness is vital and continuing today.

These two new congregations average more than 100 in worship today, and the parallel congregation has received city-wide recognition for its ministry among the homeless.

Restart

Sometimes a congregation has just had too much change or conflict, and the best thing to do is to start something new. A restart is not as easy as it sounds, as the "new" church is using the facility of the former congregation, which just closed. The new congregation often has the reputation of the former church to contend with for many years.

In a restart, you formally close the congregation. You remove historical documents, announce to the community the church is closing, and fire the pastor and key leaders from their areas of responsibility.

Then, sometime later, you open a new congregation in the space that is relevant to the context. This new church gets all of the assets of the former church, including the building.

New Directions Christian Church, which I have mentioned previously, was a restart that was done extremely well. The new church occupied space given to them by the closing Winchester Heights Christian Church, and it led to a congregation that averages thousands in worship today. It was a matter of closing an Anglo church that had little relevance in its largely African American community, and starting a new church that met the needs of the area with an effective planter.

A Word about Mergers

Merging two congregations is a redevelopment strategy. I hate to say it, but I am not a big fan of mergers. Mergers are usually the blending of two congregations who have failed to adapt to their changing context. I have never encouraged this model. I believe that past behavior is a good indicator of future behavior. If a church has failed to adapt, what leads us to believe that twice as many people who have not adapted previously will change the situation?

The landscape of our denomination is littered with dozens of mergers that have prolonged the death of failing congregations. Lyle Schaller has said that within the first two years of a merger, both congregations have 15 percent fewer members and 15 percent less financial support.[9] Recent experience would lead me to believe the percentage is higher than that.

I do not have a positive anecdote to tell regarding mergers. However, intuition tells me that several principles must exist to make this kind of congregation work. First, the congregations should be merging as a result of their strength, not because they are weak. Second, mergers work better when three congregations merge rather than just two. And third, mergers *might* have a chance if all congregations were to leave their former facilities and create a new space that relates to the new congregation's vision.

Closing Is an Option

If you think about it, every church that the Apostle Paul started has closed. In Corinth the population moved to the east, and the place where those Christians met is now isolated ruins. In Ephesus, the river silted up, and the town no longer exists. Paul was a really good church planter, but times change.

Sometimes closing is the *best* option. If a church takes a long, hard look at itself and discovers it is not very passionate about anything, is "best at" very little or nothing, and has very few human and financial resources for its ministry, then closing is an excellent option.

Nothing is more demoralizing for new church planters than to see underperforming congregations in their communities. These churches have way more resources than the new starts have, but reach very few people. Meanwhile, the church plant struggles to find the resources it needs to minister to the new people it is attracting.

In my very first year at Church Extension, I traveled with Jim Powell, our president, to witness his work as a consultant. Jim is a tremendous consultant, and I marvel every time I watch him work. However, the most memorable consultation did not go so well.

We were asked to meet with a congregation that had been declining for more than twenty years. When we drove to the church, I noted that it was the exact kind of community where you would want to develop a new church. It had a strong retail core and was busting with the construction of new housing.

Then we got to the church. It was on a triangular piece of land wedged between a park filled with young children playing soccer and a Starbucks coffee shop full of young adults who were just starting their professional lives. Across the street was a large "high end" condo that showed the last unit had sold before construction had been completed.

Yet the church was built in 1910 and almost appeared to be haunted. It was Victorian in style, with an old windmill on top and leaded glass that obviously let the wind in. In the church basement, we met with eleven of the grouchiest people I had ever met.

They had just been presented a proposal from a developer for their property. It was for $7 million, well above the church's market value. I was shocked by their reaction to what would have been a no-brainer for me. They would not give up their church building. The pastor melted down in the meeting and said some things that may not have been helpful. People called each other names, and it all went downhill.

Jim pulled everyone back together and demonstrated what this amount of money would allow the church to do. By developing a fund, they could continue to worship in rented space and have a full-time pastor, while starting two new churches a year for a very long time. They would have nothing to do with it. It was *their* church after all!

When a congregation believes the church belongs to *them,* they have lost their ability to ever have a meaningful ministry. The church belongs to Jesus Christ for the purpose of the Great Commission. There is no biblical evidence that the church was created to satisfy the needs of just a few people.

As believers in the resurrection, why do we struggle with the concept of new life following the death of a congregation if the assets are used wisely? The long-term, capital gain of a congregation should always be transferred toward creating something new. Unfortunately, many times when congregations close, the assets are used for operating expenses of some parachurch organization's operating budget. That asset is quickly consumed, and the witness of that congregation ends with the organization's next budget cycle. To me, the only meaningful way a congregation can close is if their assets are used to start a new witness that will provide the meaningful experiences they have had for a new group of people.

Great congregations go beyond remaining stagnant year after year. Great congregations know who they are and why they exist. They know what they are passionate about; they understand what they are best at in the world; and they have mobilized their resources to ensure their mission is accomplished.

Questions for Discussion

1. What would you identify as our congregation's deepest passion?
2. What would you say our congregation is "best at" in the world?
3. What human conditions exist in our community that our congregation should consider providing superior ministry toward?
4. Do you believe this church has the human and financial resources to be a *great* church?
5. When you consider this church's location on the life-cycle curve, do you think we are a candidate for a new church, missional revisioning, or redevelopment option?

5

Called for a Particular Purpose

Our image of our congregation's future ministry has now passed through the large lens of our macro view. The image has been reflected through a prism that thoughtfully considered our community, and then a final prism that reflected upon our congregation. The image then passed through a fixed eyepiece that helped us to evaluate our congregation's passion, energy, and resources. Now we come to the final lens, which twists so that you can precisely focus on an image for the future.

While this is not the first lens, it is the one closest to the viewer. Without this lens we cannot focus the image of our future ministry. This is the lens that allows us the time to reflect on what is important for a congregation, and it helps us distinguish between being a social club or a social work delivery network.

The final eyepiece of our binoculars is our biblical and theological reflection on the nature and purpose of the church. This is what some people call "missiology." Most books begin with this reflection, but I have chosen to reflect on it *after* we have viewed our world, community, and the congregation. After looking at your context, the question now becomes "what does God have in mind for this place?"

Usually congregations start with their situation and try to force a vision that will fit the church's needs. It is clear to me that this is a mistake. I can think of a number of churches that have focused on the first four lenses without considering the call from God. They wind up with missions that focus on paying people to attend church, or

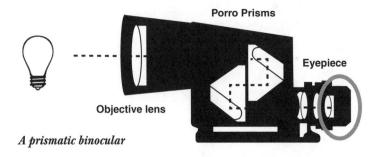

A prismatic binocular

gimmicks such as contests with prizes or parties that attract people. But the churches never invite newcomers into a true community that seeks the call of God. Ministry planning keeps at the forefront that we are a *ministry,* not a social agency or club.

To me the best planning processes start with the very large view and continue to narrow and narrow until the congregation can find its most powerful reason for existence. But by starting with the spiritual view, we may forget its importance by the time we get to the end of the process. By making this the final lens, we have the most important filter at the freshest point of the process.

It was my pleasure to have dinner with John Davis, pastor of Greenfield Christian Church in Indiana. John's congregation has transformed from a conflicted, smaller congregation that had just gone through a *very* short pastorate of his predecessor. In just three years the congregation doubled in worship attendance. During the course of our meal I asked John, "What would you say is the factor that led to such dramatic change?"

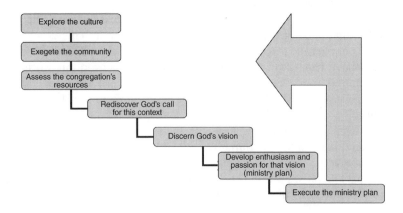

John lit up like a Christmas tree: "I came into ministry late in life. I grew up in this community, and I realize I don't have a lot of time to share the Gospel. I want to use every moment I have left in life to preach Jesus."

I know that some people may have trouble with the language John was using, but you should know that he is theologically liberal. We talked about the many social ills in his community, but it all came back to one thing: Preaching Christ. John can see that the teachings of Jesus make a big difference in people's lives and that churches need to focus on keeping "the main thing, the main thing."[1]

As I reflect on this conversation and conversations I have had with other transformative pastors, two things stand out. First, transformative pastors have a rootedness in the Gospel and can see that the Christian message makes a big difference in people's lives. Second, they have a sense of urgency about getting that message out, and convey that urgency to their congregants.

I met David Emory, another transformative pastor, who has had an exceptional ministry at his church in Middleton, Kentucky, where the congregation is exploding with growth. As he showed me his church on his day off, he said what I had heard many times before: "God is making a big difference here."

David introduced me to the people of his congregation by saying, "This is so and so; she is the absolute finest sixth-grade Sunday school teacher in the world…" No matter where we went, or who we met, David was clear that God was using the gifts of talented people to make a difference.

Both David and John have a clear sense that God is at the center of ministry—not social need, not human relations. The creator is our sense and purpose for being church. *Social services and human relations are the by-product of people who have been moved by God. And Jesus Christ clearly makes a difference in this formula.*

While the vision, mission, and values of a congregation are important, it is this type of passion that makes the largest difference. We are not "doing church" to provide a nice place for people to stop by before they go to brunch. We are about making a difference, and highly effective congregations have a sense of urgency about making that difference.

As the New Church Ministry team of the Christian Church (Disciples of Christ) has traveled, we have met and assessed many people who have a desire to become new church planters. In talking with hundreds of people, we have identified some who really know and understand the "mechanics" of church planting yet are not motivated by the spiritual and theological implications of this kind of ministry. They are captivated by the idea of planting a congregation, but not because it connects God with people. They love the concept of an "enterprise."

We had an interview with one such potential planter. While he could quote Bill Easum and Jim Griffith, he could not tell us of a time in the past fifteen years when he had had a significant conversation with someone who was not a part of a church. He had been so wrapped up in the church culture, and isolated from the "real" world, that he had not had those encounters, nor had he sought out any of those encounters. Effective planters, as well as transformative pastors, have a sense that God makes the great difference, and they desire to share that with any and every one.

A study by the Ecumenical Partners in Outreach took a close look at 400 of the nation's top new church planters. They found some strong behavioral correlations between the planters who developed strong sustainable congregations and those who did not. We discovered that the strong planters, almost to the person, when talking about their new church used language about how "God did it." They saw their role as facilitator to getting a message out, a message that is well beyond our total understanding.

In contrast, those who did not develop strong congregations felt that it was "their job" to start a church. They labored hard to make it their own rather than relying on the infinite sources that only God can give.

I will never forget that when I had was a new church planter, our congregation suffered a number of setbacks. I was in my third year, and we lost the school where we were worshiping. This forced us to nest in a congregation outside of our target area. Our congregation nested in another congregation's facility. The nesting congregation was in conflict and often blamed our congregation for minor problems in the building.

We were having a Halloween party with our children, and I had just gotten a lecture from an older woman from the host congregation about the evils of Halloween and her dismay that a church would even consider such an event. I was a bit "steamed" as a result of the conversation, but I excused myself because I was needed in the other room for the party. When I get fried like that, I have discovered it is a good time to just quietly sit, reflect, and pray; otherwise I get cynical and say something I regret. So I sat in the outer circle of people at the party.

As I sat there, I looked upon this room full of people who were total strangers to one another just three years earlier. They were executives, engineers, accountants, school administrators, social workers, computer technicians, and software engineers. They didn't work in the same companies, nor have a similar education, even though they were fairly homogenous socioeconomically. They were totally different people who had one thing and only one thing in common: their love of Jesus Christ.

I became very aware that this church was not about me and my skills as a pastor. It was about Christ and his ability to transform culture. Even a couple thousand of years after his crucifixion Jesus was still gathering crowds.

I am not a Greek scholar, but I did study it for a year in seminary. One of the Greek words for church is *ekklesia*. Paul is the one using this term 99 percent of the time it appears in scripture. It is almost always rendered as meaning "church." However, the term means specifically *an assembly of people who have been summoned for a particular purpose.*[2] While it is much shorter to just say "church," I appreciate the term's expanded meaning. The Christians were summoned for a particular *purpose*. Let us explore the scriptures for hints about what that *purpose* might be.

Commissions from Jesus

When we review the saying source material from Jesus, we find that he gave us some specific directions regarding the church and its purpose. These passages are extremely familiar to all of us, and you have likely heard many sermons on each of these. Therefore, I am using Eugene Peterson's *The Message* as the version of scripture for this book so you can begin to see these familiar passages in new ways.

The most famous of commissions from Jesus is the Great Commission, which is found in Matthew 28:18-20.

> Jesus, undeterred, went right ahead and gave his charge: "God authorized and commanded me to commission you: Go out and train everyone you meet, far and near, in this way of life, marking them by baptism in the threefold name: Father, Son, and Holy Spirit. Then instruct them in the practice of all I have commanded you. I'll be with you as you do this, day after day after day, right up to the end of the age."

I am struck by the earlier part of this chapter in Matthew, where the followers of Jesus are confused following the resurrection. It is not difficult to imagine how they were not only trying to make sense of the resurrection, but wondering about what they were supposed to do. Jesus summoned the group for a particular purpose and commissioned all of us as coworkers.

Commissioning is a way of empowering and giving permission. While congregations commission people all the time, we often fail to really empower people with the very thing Jesus calls us to do, namely making disciples. People who bring others into relationship with Christ and the church are reproductive Christians. Congregations will often say they empower, but if they never develop new leaders, or if they micromanage those they have invited to lead, the congregants will never feel fully empowered. The people of the congregation must feel they have the skills and gifts to participate in the Great Commission.

I once watched an interesting exchange in a former congregation. A new participant volunteered to provide cookies for the coffee hour following church. I watched this new participant from a distance as she carefully arranged the table with her lovingly baked offering. She even added a nice centerpiece and thematic napkins. A longer term member who had done coffee hour many times before began to quickly rearrange her table before the congregants came, and a small argument began to escalate. It became as if all peace in the world was dependent on where the chocolate chips were placed in relation to the coffee pot.

It was sad, because we commissioned yet we really didn't give her permission to do it her own way. This is a trite example of something that happens frequently in congregations and denominational structures. We are much better at trying to control things than at empowering others to do them.

Yet empowering is what Jesus calls us to do. Empower others by sending them out into the world to introduce people to the Gospel, and then lett those new people go out into the world to introduce more people and equip them, etc.

The Great Commission is a circular, not linear, process. It involves attracting, connecting, and equipping people who also attract, connect, and equip.

Mark 16:14–16 has a slightly different pronouncement from Jesus.

> Still later, as the Eleven were eating supper, he appeared and took them to task most severely for their stubborn unbelief, refusing to believe those who had seen him raised up. Then

he said, "Go into the world. Go everywhere and announce the Message of God's good news to one and all."

In Mark, the eleven are given a stern lecture regarding their unbelief. Then Jesus tells them to go everywhere and announce the message of God's good news. Jesus is clear that the church has a mission outside of itself. That mission is active, and it involves going somewhere.

There are two basic forms of evangelism: passive and active. Passive systems receive something without initiating any action. For example, windows can act as passive heat for a house in the winter. Sunlight comes through the glass and heats the home without costing the resident anything. Passive evangelism is putting up a sign, or building a unique building, or even sending out a flyer inviting people to a church. It is good evangelism, but the church receives new people with no initiation on the part of any person in the church.

Active systems require initiation. A furnace is an active heating system within a house. It requires a signal to start and requires fuel to keep it going, and it has a cost involved. Active evangelism actually means people have to talk to others.

May I be honest here? People have used embarrassing ways of sharing their faith with others. I once answered the door at my home and was met by an individual who started by saying; "Good afternoon. Did you know that you are going to hell?" My response to him was "Oh...are you God? Because I thought that was God's job to determine." (The conversation went downhill from there.) What an embarrassing way to present our faith to anyone.

People are comfortable talking about anything. They will share with friends information about their finances, where to find good movies or doctors, even intimate information about their sex lives. Talking about faith is a different matter. I have seen grown men sweat at the prospect of sharing anything about their faith. It appears to be a very private matter.

Cynthia Hale, pastor of Ray of Hope Christian Church in Atlanta, had a unique solution to that problem of shyness. One Sunday she announced that there would be a class on evangelism at the church. The nursery would be available, and a light dinner would be served.

That evening people showed up to the church with their Bibles, ate a meal, checked their children into the nursery, and then went to the classroom to learn about evangelism. They were surprised when Hale told them to get their coats on and get on the buses outside.

When they got on the bus they heard Hale announce that the children were safe, and that they would be going to the mall and that the bus would not return until each person had talked with at least three people about their faith.

As you can imagine, this was not the kind of experience her parishioners were hoping for. You see, they wanted to *study* evangelism, not necessarily *do* it. But Jesus was clear to his followers: the time to study is over; it is time to get on the bus.

Foreshadowing Acts 2, Luke 24:45–49 says:

> He went on to open their understanding of the Word of God, showing them how to read their Bibles this way. He said, "You can see now how it is written that the Messiah suffers, rises from the dead on the third day, and then a total life-change through the forgiveness of sins is proclaimed in his name to all nations—starting from here, from Jerusalem! You're the first to hear and see it. You're the witnesses. What comes next is very important: I am sending what my Father promised to you, so stay here in the city until he arrives, until you're equipped with power from on high."

In this commission, Jesus reminds us that we are the witnesses, starting here, starting now. Then he promises that there will be resources from God coming soon. We can guess that the resource is the Holy Spirit, which visits the church in Jerusalem.

Jesus hints here that without the Holy Spirit, fulfilling the commission will be impossible. A witness that is just an intellectual exercise or a job requirement is not enough. The future witness is about having soul, about having a passion within that only God can give to those who ask for it.

It is ironic that in the gospel of Luke, Jesus predicts his death and resurrection a number of times. In Mark, Jesus predicts his death and resurrection three times. Still, the disciples had no clue that his resurrection would occur. It was like they didn't hear a thing Jesus said during their time with him.

Those of us who claim to be disciples today have heard the resurrection story dozens if not hundreds of times, and we take it for granted. We have witnessed dozens if not hundreds of times the ways in which our faith community makes a difference in people's lives as well. Yet we keep it to ourselves out of concern we might offend someone by inviting him or her to join us at the well of life.

In this commission, Jesus outlines his ministry plan for the future. You are my witnesses. Get equipped by the Holy Spirit, and tell others what you know. You will receive your power from "on high".

John 20:20–22 reads:

> The disciples, seeing the Master with their own eyes, were exuberant. Jesus repeated his greeting: "Peace to you. Just as the Father sent me, I send you." Then he took a deep breath and breathed into them. "Receive the Holy Spirit," he said.

The gospel of John has a very simple yet poetic view. By passing the peace, Jesus reminds us he was sent by God to reconcile the world. He is empowering the disciples to witness as he had witnessed. John also symbolizes the passing of the Holy Spirit through the breath of Jesus. In the synoptic gospels we have lots of words, but in John, we have an actual commissioning that involves a symbolic act of passing the peace and passing the Holy Spirit.

Church life is filled with many rites of passage. From the dedication or baptism of babies, to pastors' classes or communicant classes, to marriage and even to death. The church is a place of recognizing the passages of life. These rites, when demonstrated in church life, have tremendous meaning for individuals at each stage.

When I was in the sixth grade moving to seventh, my congregation gave me a Bible. It was a real Bible, not the kids Bible I had used earlier. (This one had no pictures.) It was not bound very well, but nonetheless it became my source for learning the stories of our faith. I still have that Bible more than forty years later, and it serves as a constant reminder that I am on my faith journey, supported by a group of fellow believers.

Rites of passage are tremendously helpful in human development. They enable a person to move from one stage of life to another and symbolize the movement of life. When we take these rites of passage for granted, we cheapen the rite for the individuals who go through it.

One of my favorite moments as a pastor was when someone made a decision to claim Christ as Lord. I never had more joy than in those moments in my ministry. The more the person struggled with that decision, the more joyful it was for me to experience. What bothered me was that when we shook their hands and welcomed them in our tradition, I was always asking myself...now what do we do?

When people in our different traditions make an adult decision to follow Christ, we need to be about the business of commissioning them, not just accepting them to a church roll. There needs to be a next step.

Early Church Behavior

When we look at the book of Acts in the New Testament, we see emerging behaviors by the early church. Starting with the very first chapter in Acts, we see the people who were gathered for a particular purpose devoting themselves to prayer and taking action so that they can get organized by electing Matthias to take the place of Judas. Then one day in Jerusalem the Holy Spirit arrives, just as promised, and the first Pentecost arrives, with the church adding believers in the thousands.

> That day about three thousand took him at his word, were baptized and were signed up. They committed themselves to the teaching of the apostles, the life together, the common meal, and the prayers. Everyone around was in awe—all those wonders and signs done through the apostles! And all the believers lived in a wonderful harmony, holding everything in common. They sold whatever they owned and pooled their resources so that each person's need was met. They followed a daily discipline of worship in the Temple followed by meals at home, every meal a celebration, exuberant and joyful, as they praised God. People in general liked what they saw. Every day their number grew as God added those who were saved. (Acts 2:41–47)

Don't you just love this image of the church? It portrays people living together in harmony, caring for one another, worshiping every day, and ending the day with a joyful and celebrative meal. But more importantly, they were growing in their faith every day. People were sharing their joy with others. They were passionate about their faith and what they had witnessed. They couldn't keep it a secret. Even though they were living in a real oppressive society, they let the word out. They were evangelists.

Caring and reaching out were at the very center of the church.

The New Testament presents other pictures of the early church. From the people who were drinking too much wine at early communion meals in Corinth, to the church of Antioch and the way they sent out missionaries, there are many hints about the practices and beliefs of that early church:

- Baptism of believers
- Sharing common meals
- Preaching the truth of God
- Teaching
- Worshiping and celebrating
- Healing
- Praying
- Sending out people for mission

The early church had a social aspect, but it was always centered around proclaiming Jesus and waiting for his return. Martha Grace Reese, in her *Unbinding the Gospel* series, has uncovered this essential truth.[3] Congregations that are transformed do not spend time just studying demographics and marketing techniques. They rediscover the living Christ and deepen their relationship with God.

Can Congregations Be Redeemed?

As you may recall earlier in this book, we discussed Theory U and intimated how it described a process of redemption. It raises the issue about redeeming congregations. I am sure that congregations can be redeemed if they carefully examine the "will" of the congregation.

I was reading the book of Samuel and discovered a small portion that I had not examined before in 1 Samuel 17. The story has a lot of drama even before David takes on the giant Goliath. David, who is the youngest of his family and a fairly small young man, has the courage to volunteer to take on this giant who made the other Israelites shake in their boots. King Saul, who by now is getting older, either sees something in David or is left with no other options because none of the other Israelites volunteer to take on the giant. Saul agrees to let David represent Israel.

This was a pretty shaky moment for Israel. If David failed, the Philistines could have their way with them, not only taking their land, but their lives as well. Knowing that Israel was totally dependent on David, Saul gives him his own tunic, dresses him in armor, and provides a helmet. Then he arms him with a large sword that David could hardly lift.

King Saul was applying the methods of past success as a way of coaching David. Armor had worked well for Israel as they forged their way in battles with other enemy armies. But the match between David and the giant was a very different kind of battle, and the weapons of the past would have led to disaster.

The young David discovers he cannot maneuver in the heavy armor. He cannot lift the sword out of its belt. In the most pivotal part of the story, he recognizes that using this armor would be a large disadvantage for him, takes it off, and finds five smooth stones for his sling in the nearby *wadi* (stream). This single decision led to victory for the young man. He used what he was "best at" (a sling) to take on the giant, rather than what someone else placed on him as a mantle of former successes.

Ministry planning can be successful if a church uses its best tools for taking on its "giants." In our metaphor, the giant is the context in which you are doing ministry (worldview and community). It is up to we Davids to use the tools our congregation has ("best at" and other resources), and doing what we know how to do best (proclaiming Christ), *if we have the courage and the will.*

As you recall in our earlier conversation about life-cycle, Theory U[4] requires a congregation's opening their mind to new possibilities, opening their heart to their context and their neighbors, while finally making a decision, which means opening their will.

I have worked with many congregations that cannot get past the opening of their minds. They can look at data related to their congregation and their community and talk it to death, but in the end they cannot feel the compassion that Jesus has for the people around them and they fail to ignite passion about the community. A congregation that cannot engage its heart will never experience the joy of an authentic Christian community. Any ministry plan that does not go deeper than this will fail.

I have witnessed congregations that have a deep compassion for those around the world and in their community as well. These congregations will study the mission field and pray reverently for those in need. I visited a congregation that had a 60,000 square-foot building filled with a food pantry, clothes pantry, and much more, but the congregation only averaged fifteen in worship. They provided a dinner each week for the community that more than 100 would attend, but they did not preach Christ. A mind and a heart are not enough for becoming a vital congregation, it requires our "will." What will we do for the sake of Christ?

David Emory of Middleton, Kentucky, says it best. "Jesus never preached his opinions; he preached his convictions." To turn that concept slightly, the task of vital congregations is not about forming opinions, but about leading people to convictions that lead toward a deeper experience with the creator.

A key aspect of the story of David is that he had the will and the courage to accept the challenge of the giant in front of him. He also had the wisdom to use the tools and skills that God had given him rather than trying to use the things that brought success in other times. David is one of the early heroes of the Bible.

Within mythology is the basic plot line of the "journey of the hero." This plot line comes from deep within the human psyche and is portrayed not only in secular mythology and legends from other cultures but also within scripture. The journey of the hero involves separation from the community, trial, and then victory. This plot is similar in literature from the Iliad, to the gospels, to the plot line of any good movie today. A hero is one who moves to a deeper understanding of truth, accepts a challenge, struggles, and then enjoys a victory.

In the Christian context, the Bible has many examples of heroes, from Noah through the sufferings of Paul. However, the central story of our faith is that of Jesus, who separates himself from his community when he goes to the dessert and faces his temptations. Jesus emerges from the desert and begins a ministry with his disciples (a core team), which leads to trials and struggles that culminate in his victory of resurrection.

What is curious is that most of us take the story of redemption to be personal in nature, while in the biblical context salvation means clearly the redemption of God's people. Redemption is communal. This means that if a congregation considers itself to be a group of God's people, it can be redeemed.

In every story the hero is always way out in front of the people. The hero separates from the community and takes a view of it from 30,000 feet. He or she then goes through the process of thinking and feeling until emerging with a sense of "will" that comes from interior courage.

In a ministry-planning concept, this means taking a different kind of journey for a congregation. This process, which is outlined in the next chapter, is that of leading people to a place they would not have naturally gone. It involves getting out of the armor of the past and finding the tools that will propel the people of God toward that which they are called to be.

When we add Theory U next to the life-cycle of a congregation, you see the path of redemption for congregations. It involves the separation of the congregation, allowing for a period of reflection much like Jesus did in the wilderness. It involves congregations moving through the data about the community and the church in a rational, analytical way (thinking); moving to numerous conversations about what this might mean (feeling); and finally making a decision about what to do about it. Sometimes the congregation cannot make that journey together, but a

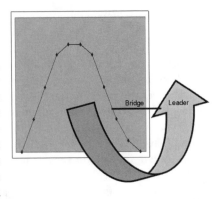

leader can inspire them to decide. Essentially it comes down to the question: "What *will* we do for the cause of Christ?" (Not "what *can* we do for the cause of Christ?")

Most heroes surround themselves with others. Jesus surrounded himself with disciples. While these co-leaders could only begin to get a glimpse of God's realm, they served as valuable bridges between the community and the leader. These "bridge" people help bring the community to a new way of being. This is why effective ministry planning uses the gifts of a small group on behalf of the community.

Congregations that use the armor of the past tend to group themselves in one or two of four domains. Congregations tend to gravitate toward one domain over the others without giving consideration to the balanced nature of the early church.

Four Domains of Effective Faith

Israel Galindo makes a distinction between "faith" and "effective faith":

Effective faith is the kind of faith that makes a difference, has an effect, on the way we live our lives.[5]

He states that everyone has faith. They might have faith in government, faith in science, faith in themselves. But effective faith has an overt impact on our lives, the way we behave, the way we think and make decisions. There are four domains of effectual faith:

- Affective (feelings, emotions, values)
- Cognitive (knowledge, understanding, comprehension)
- Behavioral (actions, conduct, skills)
- Volitional (will, conviction, intentionality)[6]

Effective faith will have a bit of all four elements. Congregations also shape the spirituality of their participants in these four ways. These domains are the hidden values of a congregation, as Galindo would say,[7] and it is important for individuals and congregations to have a balance of these domains in their lives.

Affective Congregations

Affective congregations lean on emotion and feelings to help people discover their path toward God. At their worst, they are extremely emotive, but they can capture a sense of the mystical nature of God that is beyond our explaining. They effectively use music as a form of centering people, and engage people in seriously considering their values.

While working on my seminary degree I was able to visit Glide Memorial Church in San Francisco. This congregation has been led by the Rev. Cecil Williams for many years and has a profound ministry among the people of the Tenderloin district. Its ministry was featured in the movie *The Pursuit of Happyness,* which shows the impact of this congregation on one man's life when he and his young son became homeless.

While the church is sometimes controversial, there is no question that this congregation is serious about making a difference in people's lives, and that no matter who you are, you are loved and welcomed at Glide Memorial. Worshiping with the congregation is a liberating experience for anyone who attends. For me, as an uptight white guy, I felt just as accepted as the transgendered Hispanic person who sat next to me. The church affirms that class, race, economic status, and other labels mean nothing in the kingdom of God.

The music is moving beyond belief. I remember a solo about wanting to know what love is that was sung by a middle-aged man who worked in the financial district. It was followed by a moving testimony and sermon. At the end of worship the congregation sang the *Battle Hymn of the Republic* in a way I had never experienced. No longer a war song, it focused on our eyes seeing the glory of the Lord. The walking bass line and rhythm kept going long after the service ended, and people stayed and danced in the aisles, high-fiving visitors and expressing unbridled joy.

I remember this service like it was yesterday even though I attended there in 1978.

Carl Jung, the great psychologist who was a contemporary of Freud, had a powerful understanding of the human psyche. While

Freud only understood that humans were emotional and rational, Jung understood spirituality. Jung also recognized the spiritual nature of a human being and saw that spirituality transformed people in ways that defied logic.[8] While this is an oversimplification, it is a basic truth that the church confirms.

Spirituality can help people through difficult illnesses and losses. Spirituality can enable a person to overcome weakness, while our rationality might not allow us to overcome it. When we allow the secular world to reduce the church to either rational or emotional, the church becomes polarized. I believe that if we fail to explore our feelings as a part of our spiritual journey, then we will miss a great opportunity for spiritual growth.

Cognitive Congregations

Cognitive congregations focus on knowing God through study, memorization, and reflection. Cognitive congregations focus on classroom study. They enjoy formal settings for conversations, papers on theology, and teaching the faith. Worship in cognitive congregations will explore silence, sing music as it is written, and favor a classical traditional approach to understanding God. Preaching is important in this kind of church, and knowing God is equal to understanding the faith. These congregations could be either liberal or conservative.

The educational processes of these congregations lead people through all their stages of understanding God. For these congregations, the message must make a direct connection with everyday life so that participants can understand the nature of God at work in their lives. Strictly cognitive congregations will reject anything that has to do with emotion. Emotion is seen as manipulation.

One of my most embarrassing moments came when I was preaching at a cognitive congregation. I love to lace humor into my sermons and was giving the message my very best. I thought I was pretty funny, but when I looked out into the congregation there wasn't even a smile, let alone a chuckle. I began to fear I had offended somebody or said something inappropriate. This tempered my delivery for the rest of the message, and I found myself pretty much sticking to the script and feeling poorly about what I had done in worship that day.

As church members left the church, they were enthusiastic about the sermon. One man told me on the way out he had not laughed that hard in years. I was totally confused because that man in particular looked like he was about to shoot me when I was preaching. Then I realized: *This is a cognitive church, and any display of emotion is inappropriate, including laughter.* The man would hurt himself containing laughter rather than express it openly in that setting.

Behavioral Churches

Behavioral churches are focused on getting people to behave as they believe Jesus would have us behave. Talk of sin and punishment are hallmarks of these congregations. These kinds of congregations will get into details about how you can get right with God and also point a lot to the folly of other sinners who cannot tow the line. They are clear about who is going to heaven and who is not. The purpose for being a part of this faith community is so "you can get it right."

I think you can tell I'm not a big fan of this kind of church. To me, there are just too many parallels between these faith communities and the Pharisees in the New Testament.

Volitional Congregations

According to Wikipedia, *volition* or will is the cognitive process by which an individual decides on and commits to a particular course of action.[9] It is a purely linear approach to faith, with specific steps. It is defined as purposive striving. This kind of congregation has a specific process by which a person can enter and grow in faith.

I met a man on a flight who engaged me in one of the most frustrating conversations I have ever had. Even though he knew I was a person of faith, he was insistent on leading me through a conversation that was in his notebook. He would come to a page in which he would ask me a question. If I answered wrong, we would have to stay on that page and list all the reasons I was wrong. Eventually I would agree with him so I could move to the next page. (I'm agenda driven and wanted to see where this was leading me.)

This was an example of a volitional process. It suggested that there is only one path by which I can come into relationship with Christ. Other congregations like this will have a specific course of study that congregants must participate in in order to move to the next stage of development. You cannot be a leader in these settings without having completed a certain number of levels in training.

Strictly volitional congregations leave most of us cold. To me they limit the immense ability of God to reach people.

While traveling in China with a group of new church pastors, I met a young Chinese woman who was a professional model flying from Xian to Beijing. She discovered we were Christian ministers and wanted to know more about Christianity. China did not allow for free expression of religion until the end of the Cultural Revolution (about 1966–1976). Today the church in China is exploding with growth. I enjoyed watching my colleagues as they shared with her. Their faces lit up, and they were doing what they loved doing more than anything in the world–inviting someone into the faith. As we parted her company at the airport, we invited her to join us in worship that Sunday in Beijing.

As new church pastors, we invite people to church all the time. Only about one person out of fifty ever joins us. That Sunday, to our amazement, that young woman came to her very first Christian worship service. I was lucky to sit by her during worship and watch her reaction as she looked at a hymnal for the first time, as she participated in corporate prayer for the first time.

What gave us all the most joy was giving her a Bible. A pastor in the group gave the woman his Chinese-English Bible as a gift to remind her of our encounter. I watched her during church open the Bible and thumb through its pages with wonderment. She went to the contents and studied the names of all the books in the Bible with little understanding about what any of those strange title names would mean.

I then thought about how many of our churches do nothing to help people move from being first introduced to the faith to actually maturing in the faith. Few congregations have a process. We expect people to know a lot about the faith before ever participating in our faith community.

I once took a group of youth Christmas caroling in a senior citizens' home. I didn't bring song sheets; I just figured we would sing the first verse and move to the next carol. I was shocked to discover as we practiced at the church that these young people did not know the words to carols. They knew "Rudolf the Red-Nosed Reindeer," but knew very few of the carols that had anything to do with the birth of Jesus. As I ran off song sheets, it dawned on me. I learned my carols at school as well as the church. They don't teach carols at school anymore (something I agree with). Teaching carols is the job of the church, and we are not doing a very good job sometimes.

If our congregations are balanced, we will have elements that allow for people to grow in the faith. James Fowler in his famous work *Stages of Faith* helps us with a roadmap of the ways in which people develop in their quest for human meaning. Based on the works of sociologists such as Piaget and Kohlberg, Fowler's work maps the path that we share in human experience.[10] In reviewing his book I notice how little we do in most churches to bring people through that process.

Fowler's Stage	Task
Intuitive-Projective Faith	Learning to imitate faith
Mythic-Literal Faith	The taking on of the communal stories and making them their own
Synthetic-Conventional Faith	Seeing the world through peers, and adopting the community's values
Individuative-Reflective Faith	The act of questioning the community's values to make them your own
Conjunctive Faith	Development of self-awareness and life principles
Universalizing Faith	Integrating that self-awareness with the principles of other faiths

Congregations have people in every one of these stages of development. Most congregations do a very good job helping people through the first four stages, but we often fail at helping folks move through the last two, to develop a truly mature faith that lifts up others.

In summary, congregations are called together for a particular purpose, namely equipping people so they can mature in the faith and witness to the ends of the earth. We are not called to develop a social club or even a social service agency. Instead, through worship, prayer, service, and sharing common meals, we equip people who cannot help but share the good news of Jesus Christ.

The output of congregations that pursue that purpose is people who are engaged in loving relationships with one another, with their community contex,t and with the entirety of creation. The congregation helps people work through their stages of faith development, empowering them to be Christ's witnesses from Jerusalem to the ends of the earth.

Questions for Discussion

1. When we look at the "commissioning" passages from the gospels, what common themes appear?
2. Which of the three tasks (attract, connect, and equip) would you say our congregation excels in?

3. When you consider the following list of activities of the early church, is there anything missing from our church today? What does our church do that is not on the list?

> • Baptism of believers
> • Sharing common meals
> • Preaching the story of God
> • Teaching
> • Worshiping a celebrating
> • Healing
> • Praying
> • Sending out people for mission

4. What are the elements of the "journey of the hero"? Has our congregation been engaged in this journey, or do we tend to put on the armor of the past?

5. Of the four domains [affective (feelings, emotions, values); cognitive (knowledge, understanding, comprehension); behavioral (actions, conduct, skills); volitional (will, conviction, intentionality], which describes our church best?

6. Do we take "faith development stages" into consideration for the ordering of our church life together?

6

Writing a Ministry Plan

We have talked a lot about the binoculars as a tool for looking off into the future, and how you can use the things that have passed through the lens to develop a vision of the future. A vision does little good, however, without a means to communicate what you have seen. Writing a plan not only helps you communicate the vision, but the discipline allows you to refine your thinking.

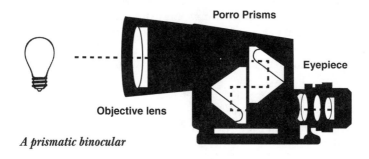

A prismatic binocular

I have talked with many church development people over the years about ministry planning. *Ministry* is such a broad term that it is difficult to understand without a systematic way of approaching planning. Most people who discuss their "ministry plan" end up discussing a "ministry idea."

Banks have required "business plans" for many years. These plans have become more formalized and have led even to the development of software that helps new small business owners develop plans they can submit to banks. A good business plan leads to capital, which enables the business to get off the ground. While there are some differences in these plans, several elements appear to be fairly consistent in business planning:

- Executive summary
- Market analysis
- Company description
- Organization and management
- Service and product line
- Funding request
- Financials
- Appendices

The business plan can easily be adapted to congregational life with some additional twists. So I am adding a format for a *Ministry Plan* as a starting point for you to use in consideration for developing your future ideas. You may wish to add categories to this process, but I would like to outline elements that I consider essential.

Before we get too far in this process, let me add that a plan needs to be written by a key leader in the congregation as a "straw dog" for conversation. This leader (often the pastor) needs to take time to reflect in prayer, research, and have many conversations with people before writing the plan. After completing a time of research, the leader would then begin to gain approval in an appropriate fashion for that congregation, one element at a time.

The reason I suggest this manner of planning is that it is too cumbersome to be completed by a committee. Writing a document with a committee is a painful process and a big waste of valuable volunteer time. It is always best to have some ideas that a group can give input to and improve on. However, the leader does need to spend time listening, not just taking their own ideas and ramming them down a congregation's throat. Let me suggest several phases in order to gather the data that you might need to write this plan:

Phase I: Conduct a series of interviews with church participants.
Phase II: Research the community.
Phase III: Assess the congregation and its ministry delivery systems.
Phase IV: Evaluate the congregation's decision-making process and use of volunteers.

Phase V: Evaluate the congregation's financial capacity.

Phase VI: Take a private retreat for prayer, reflection, and writing of the plan.

Phase VII: Get a ministry plan adopted by the congregation.

This process can take a significant amount of time (three months to a year), and must be a priority for the congregation. It is important to gain acceptance for this planning process from the appropriate group in your church, with the understanding that if the pastor is writing the plan, the church will allow the pastor time for interviews and the week of reflective writing. The church also must understand that the pastor could be excused from some duties in order to accomplish the research goals. Let's look at the tasks required for each phase

Phase I: The Series of Interviews

When I entered my fifteenth year of serving a congregation, I did some significant reflection on the future ministry of that congregation. To get to the next level of development, I created an interview process with church members that gave me a tremendous amount of information and led to some significant changes in ministry.

It wasn't always real affirming to talk with members in this straightforward fashion, but it was the best way to discover the points of engagement they had with the church and the programs that would be most helpful to them.

In the book *In Search of Excellence*[1] Thomas Peters and Robert Waterman write about ways in which companies reach excellence. They state that excellent companies keep "close to the customer." That is to say, the companies discover how the customers' needs are changing, and how their company can serve them. I think that principle applies to congregations too. We need to be with people at times *other* than at church, in crisis, or in a hospital, to discuss their lives and hear about the challenges they are facing.

The way the process worked was simple. I announced to the congregation that I would be coming to each person's home for a fifteen-minute visit over the next few months. I stated that I would not be inspecting their homes to see if they were clean and that I did not want any food or drink. I just wanted a short conversation about the future of our congregation. I also said they did not need to get out the family Bible and display it prominently, and added that it was fine with me if they would like to meet me somewhere other than their homes.

We set up sign-up sheets with four spots for three nights a week over the next three months. There was another sign-up sheet for those available during the day.

We took those sheets and organized the times in which the interviews could take place. At the time we had sixty-five active families, and it took me just four months to conduct those interviews. On the evening interviews I would start at 7:00 p.m. and be home by 9:30. I talked with 100 percent of my active families and 60 percent of the families who were sporadic in their attendance.

Here is a possible script for such an interview:

4 min: Greetings and update on the family

Transition: "*Well, as you know we are in the process of writing a new ministry plan for our congregation. I would like to talk with you briefly about your engagement with the church and ways in which our church could better serve you and your family, because we want to facilitate your continued growth in faith.*"

2 min.: When you consider all the things you do in church, when do you feel most engaged or challenged or fulfilled? (Follow-up if appropriate—Is there something you would like to be doing but have not been asked or have not felt free to suggest?)

2 min.: What do you feel is the most valuable ministry our church offers?

2 min.: What is the one thing or event at church in which time passes quickly?

2 min.: What is the one thing in our community that seems to cry out to our church for attention?

2 min.: What do you think we should consider for our congregation's future planning?

1 min. Closing prayer for the family and for the church.

It can be challenging to keep this conversation to fifteen minutes and honor what you have asked the family for. I would occasionally have to skip a question in the middle. At other times there were awkward silences. When people could not think of times in the church where they were engaged, it said something to me, and there was no need to sit for two minutes in silence before moving to the next question.

I was amazed that people responded to "What ministry is most valuable?" with the answer of the ministry program we offered for children, regardless of whether they had children in their family or not. It told me that the congregation placed a high value on serving children.

I discovered how much volunteer resources were still available, and I also discovered the people who were close to burning out. I also learned a *lot* about areas where people thought our church could do better, especially in the last question. This was not always affirming, but very important information.

I kept the notes from the interview for later reflection and quickly moved to the next home. Sometimes a conversation would need to be continued because I had to get to the next house. It was very easy at that point to get another time for a longer conversation, usually at the church office, since they knew I was committed to seeing every household.

Phase II: Researching the Community

You can look at chapter 2 for practical ways in which you can research your community. Don't forget to interview city, county, and hospital officials in that process. Read your paper, talk with the chamber of commerce, and learn what you can. Remember there is a need to ask, observe, and research. Relying only on research without the interviews will dramatically reduce the impact of this phase.

Phase III: Assessing Your Congregation

You can look again at chapter 3 to see ways in which you can assess your congregation. If your congregation has participated in New Beginnings,© you will have had the benefit of a tightly written forty-page report on all aspects of your congregation, including facilities, finances, community gaps, and more. To learn more about New Beginnings© you can contact Church Extension if you are a Disciples of Christ congregation. Other denominations are starting to adopt this process as well. The New Beginnings© Process is a proven ministry assessment service that would greatly inform any ministry planning process.

Phase IV: Evaluating Your Congregation's Decision-making Process and Use of Volunteers

This phase is fairly simple, as it is most likely outlined in the constitution and by-laws of your congregation. Review the documents and count the number of officers required by your by-laws, then multiply that by the number of hours that are required to fulfill their duties per year.

Then list the volunteers required for the delivery of programs in the congregation over the course of the year, and the hours required for them to fulfill their duties. In doing so, you will have a list that looks something like the chart below, from an actual church that averaged fifty people in attendane on Sundays:

DECISION MAKERS	Number	Hours per month pp	Total Vh per year
Cong. President	1	4	48
Cong. VP of Programs	1	8	96
Church Treas.	1	6	72
Church Financial Sect.	1	10	120
Church Sect.	1	2	24
Elders	8	4	384
Deacons	16	1	192
Trustees	8	2	192
Property Chairman	1	10	120
Fellowship Planning Team	5	3	180
Education Committee	6	3	216
CWF Chairman	1	8	96
Total Vh per year			**1740**
PROGRAM DELIVERY VOLUNTEERS			
Youth Volunteers	2	12	288
Sunday School Teachers	4	8	384
Community Supper	4	1	48
Annual Rummage Sale	12	0.5	72
Choir	10	4	480
Fellowship Activities	8	2	192
Misc.	6	4	288
Total Vh per year			**1752**

When you compare Decision Makers Vh (Volunteer hours) to the Program Delivery Vh, you can see that they are just about even for this congregation. That means that for every volunteer hour of program delivery, a volunteer hour is required to make decisions. When you consider that this congregation only has 3,500 hours of volunteer time per year, you begin to wonder if it is wise to have such a cumbersome planning and decision-making process for a congregation of this size.

Peters and Waterman also discovered that excellent businesses had "fluidity" in the ways in which they made decisions.[2] Team leaders in these dynamic companies were empowered to make decisions on the floor, which enabled the business to take advantage of the changing marketplace in a rapid fashion. Unfortunately many congregations take too much time and engage far too many people in making decisions about small matters.

Volunteer hours are a commodity just as valuable as money and property, and it is important that congregations begin thinking more carefully how they spend those hours. The congregation above was able to free up an additional 1,000 hours of volunteer time by just shifting their board meeting to four times a year. At certain times of the year they would have to add an additional meeting, but for the most part the new system worked, and it was far easier for the congregation to recruit decision makers and program delivery volunteers.

Another consideration as you reflect on volunteers in the church is the system by which the congregation develops future leaders. Most congregations use the natural leaders and those who are not so gifted to lead in specific areas. What occurs is frustration with some in the church over the ways in which some leaders function. This leads to that leader's inability to recruit help for the tasks for which they have oversight. In many cases, the congregation will not say anything, and will instead just let that person stumble through their term.

Good congregational leaders always have an eye for future "talent." That is, people in the congregation whot could develop in a short period of time into effective leaders. For example, if a congregation is smart, they will recruit someone for a position like property chairman and have the person work with the current chair for a year with the intent of taking on the responsibility the next year.

With new congregations we have to be very careful about establishing officers too early in their development process. It takes time to identify the talented leaders in an emerging congregation. A church planter has to be able to sense the motive of that person who is eager to lead, while also being sensitive to potential leaders who are not as loud.

While serving a congregation, we once made a big mistake in that regard. We recruited a new member, who had joined six months earlier, to be our church treasurer. She had her own accounting business. We thought that writing a few checks for the church each month should be a snap for someone like that, and she willingly accepted the position. We felt good about it because we had always worked hard to engage people as soon as they became a part of our church in our rapidly shifting area.

However, she was not that committed. She had just met a man and was spending every free moment engaged in that relationship. We soon received past due notices, threats to turn off the electricity, and hefty late payment fees. We called the person, who assured us everything would be brought current, at least three times. There were no financial reports for the board, paychecks were skipped, and chaos ensued.

Finally, the vice president of the congregation drove her car to the treasurer's house and waited in the driveway until she came home, late one evening. She notified her she was no longer the treasurer and took the bills and checkbook as well as the financial records from her. The situation was embarrassing. Needless to say we lost any participation from the treasurer, who quit the church that week.

This could have been avoided if we had had a system in place for not only identifying people, but taking time to get to know them while developing their leadership skills.

More often than not we use the Kit Carson method of recruitment. If you remember your western U.S. history, Kit Carson, the famous buffalo hunter, was really not that skilled. He would ride into a herd of buffalo, and the buffalo would scatter. The sleepy or old buffalo would just lie on the ground and become Kit Carson's next target. In a way, that is how most churches recruit leaders. We announce we are looking for a junior high youth worker, and then when we enter the room, the buffalo (volunteers) scatter, and we recruit the weakest leader for the most important job.

Congregations that are serious about leader development do not recruit people because they need a warm body. They recruit people because the job is important, so important that the church is willing to invest in the development of that leader.

As you assess the congregation's decision-making process, you need to reflect on your volunteer assets and how well you use and develop them.

Phase V: Evaluating the Congregation's Financial Capacity

The three main categories for evaluating the congregation's financial capacity are Income streams for operations, operating expenses, and capital assets and liabilities.

Income Streams for Operations

Congregations separate capital income for building projects from operating income because building improvements actually add to the value of the church building, whereas operating income pays for program without affecting the congregation's net worth. Each congregation receives income from the offerings of its members and other sources. Offering income is the combination of loose offering, designated offerings, and pledged income. Identifiable gifts from congregational participants for the ministry of the church are offering income. However, offering incomet does not include offerings that are designated specifically for capital development (like a building fund).

Congregations often receive outside support in addition to offerings. This includes income from building rentals, cell phone towers, preschools, investment income, fundraisers, and so on.

At least 65 percent of the congregation's operating income should come from offering support. Congregations that receive more than that percentage from outside sources are then dependent on those sources for providing ministry.

Operating Expenses

After evaluating many church budgets,we have noticed that the patterns of spending in vital congregations differ widely from congregations that are struggling for survival. The chart below shows categories of spending and how congregations spend.

Spending Category	Vital Congregation	Struggling Congregation
All Salaries and Benefits	50%	>50%
Building and Administration Costs	25%	>25%
Program Expenses	15%	<15%
Mission Giving	10%	<10%

Salary Support

Salary support includes salaries of all church staff and the cost of their benefits, such as Social Security offsets, health insurance, pension, and so forth. It does not include costs such as auto expense or office reimbursements. Most congregations will expend about 50 percent of their income on salary support, shortchanging mission outreach and programs.

Building and Administration

These are the costs associated with running the church office and the building, such as insurance, utility bills, maintenance, and grounds upkeep. An average congregation will support building and administration costs with 25 percent of their income. Congregations that are not "ight-sized find themselves paying more for facilities, usually at the expense of their program and missions.

Program Expenses

Program costs include faith development, evangelism, and worship materials; choir music and supplies; advertising; and other resources and supplies that enable programs to operate. This is usually about 15 percent of a church's budget. Because this is the place where most congregations can control spending, they will usually decrease their spending in this category first. We have discovered many struggling congregations actually spend less than 3 percent of their income on program.

Mission Giving

Mission giving is money that the congregation has contributed to denominational mission causes as well as local mission causes. Mission giving trends are about 10 percent of a vital congregation's budget as a starting point. Congregations will often reduce their mission spending after depleting their program spending.

Capital Assets and Liabilities

Many congregations have permanent and designated funds that have been donated for specific purposes. These funds provide income for special projects, such as a new piano, or choir robes. These funds are usually placed in a restricted account for their intendedl purpose only.

I have discovered that many long-term congregations have thousands of dollars in these restricted accounts that they cannot touch, yet the use for which they were given no longer exists. One such church had accumulated $60,000 in these accounts for such things as cleaning choir robes they no longer used and tuning the pipe organ they no longer had. Congregations should give consideration to developing a policy that is understood by donors that restricted gifts will be held until spent for their specific purpose, but that after two years, the funds will be converted into operating income.

In another congregation more than 40 percent of the operating income was designated for specific things. Some people did not like the pastor and did not want their offerings supporting him in any way. Other people loved the youth program, but didn't trust the church board to financially support it. A congregation enters a very slippery slope when they allow members to share their giving in that way. It is also not the kind of stewardship that God desires.

Long-term, permanent funds need to be considered when viewing a congregation's financial streams. Healthy congregations will have these funds available for broad purposes, yet never are totally reliant on them. Many experts in the field of establishing permanent funds advise that congregations develop policies regarding these funds, even if they do not have any. With the Disciples of Christ, the Christian Church Foundation provides numerous resources to help a church create and manage these funds.

We have discovered that some congregations choose to invest these funds themselves, rather than using denominational resources. Congregations that have members who have done well in personal investing may be able to handle this. However, experience has demonstrated that this opens the door to the kinds of knuckleheads we discussed earlier. Two cases come to mind. In one, a member who was a stock trader was given the congregation's portfolio to manage. He discovered a good personal income stream by buying and selling the church's stocks, and profiting from the fees they generated. Within a short time he had effectively cost the church nearly $60,000 of their investment. A second case involved a church where the professional investor served the church well for twenty years. After he died, however, no one in the congregation understood trading and portfolio management. Several years later, many of the stocks they held were worth nothing.

Denominational fund managers also have another advantage. Most are required to invest in morally conscious ways. Most contributors to these funds would not want to see their funds invested in breweries, tobacco companies, or even multinational corporations with questionable practices in developing countries.

A major asset for a congregation is their building. It is not an asset if it is too large or has many deferred maintenance items, however. You can do an analysis of your facility with a walk-through inspection. Most congregations' property committees know exactly what needs attention if they just had the funds, and they likely know what the cost of repairs would be.

I once reviewed a facility in California that was worth $4 million. While it was valuable real estate, the small congregation was not maintaining it with their small income stream, and the building was falling more and more into disrepair. There were dozens of unused rooms with leaky roofs, falling plaster, asbestos walls, and an electrical system that was installed in 1930. It had sustained $250,000 in earthquake damage and had no assets to work with. This facility is considered a liability for a congregation averaging eleven people on Sundays.

Congregations may have debts. To evaluate your debt to operating ratio use the following formula:

(Monthly Debt X 12) / Total Annual Income = Debt Ratio

A congregation's debt ratio should never be over 38 percent. I would suggest congregations stay below 25 percent. The closer to 38 percent, the deeper the financial stress on a congregation. If a congregation has no debt, there is a financial capacity for building improvements that a congregation may have not considered.

Phase VI: Writing the Plan

Most planning processes break down because the person leading the process does not take time for reflection and writing. This cannot be done on the fly. It must be done intentionally, and in a place conducive to this kind of activity..

At the start of the process, it should be agreed that the leader is given time away from the congregation to reflect, pray, and write. Normally this process would take at least a week.

The leader should bring all the data he or she has gathered to this point, including all of the ideas generated through interviews. Then the leader must go to another place. Most church camps offer private retreat space. Some church members have cabins they would offer in the off-season. Do not bring distractions, but do bring lots of coffee.

Phase VII: Getting the Plan Adopted

Once the plan is written it would be good to submit the draft to several key individuals who are highly regarded by the congregation. You will gain from their comments and insights. Informally giving them an opportunity for early input will enable them to be more supportive of the plan in later portions of the process., and help you avoid problems once the plan becomes public.

The person who has written the ministry plan will have an enormous personal stake in what he or she has written. This is why it is so important for the writer to "back off" and take input from others.

Many congregational leaders may want to improve the plan. I have discovered that often people will get stuck on little things that really have no bearing on the overall plan. They may want to argue about the history; they may take issue with the finances or some of the math. Stay focused, for you want the ministry plan to reflect the mission that God is calling the congregation to adopt. However, this imput will often improve the plan. Remember, you are presenting a "straw dog" so that the church can then engage the process of ministry planning rather than writing a document as a committee.

It would be important then to distribute copies of the plan to the appropriate group for conversation. If it is a church board, I would get the report to them early and devote an entire meeting to discussing the plan. Changes may then occur to the draft.

Following the board's adoption, the plan is ready to be presented to the congregation. A series of meetings in homes or small groups to present and discuss the report is very important before coming to a congregational meeting. Those who are anxious about the congregation's future can use those smaller forums to discuss their ideas. More adjustments may occur during this time. The resolution to adopt the ministry plan should also include a date for implementation.

The Ministry Plan Outline

I. Executive Summary
II. Congregational History
III. Community Analysis
IV. Congregational Assessment (including growing gaps)
   a. The Congregation's Passion
   b. What Congregation Can Be "Best at"
   c. Resources Available for Ministry
      i. Financial
      ii. Leadership
      iii. Facilities
V. A Vision for the Future
   a. Vision Statement
      i. Benefit Analysis
         1. For Community
         2. For Congregation Participants
         3. For Prospective Participants
   b. Mission Statement
   c. Values Statement

Writing the Ministry Plan

I. The Executive Summary

The Executive Summary is best written after the plan is completely finished. The summary highlights the congregation's history and community's needs. It summarizes the strategy and benefits of the new ministry plan and highlights the need to accomplish the plan. It is best to keep each section at one or two pages.

II. The Congregational History

A brief history of the congregation should be outlined, as well as the attendance patterns associated with the church's history. It is always more effective if the history of the community is drawn into this narrative. Congregational high points and impacts should also be mentioned.

When mentioning the origins of the congregation, the writer should discuss the purpose for which the congregation was formed. It is important to show through this history how the community has changed and how the congregation may or may not have adapted to changes. Any contrast to the original mission of the congregation and the current setting are important.

Include core details about the past ten years, including the engagement patterns of participants. A pin map of participants in relationship to the church is also helpful. It is important to add to this section data about additions to the congregation as well as baptisms.

III. Community Analysis

Chapter 2 should give you plenty of information regarding ways you can gather data about the community. Ministry opportunities should be a hallmark of this section. Don't just mention the high number of single parents, but begin to note ways in which the church can make a difference in this setting.

IV. Congregational Assessment

This will likely be a long analysis of the congregation.

To discuss the congregation's passion and energy you can mention information that you gained in the interviews with congregants. What are they saying about their engagement in the church, as well as future engagement potential? Some reflection on the average ages of participants and the length of their tenure in the church will also give you an indication about the congregation's energy level.

Never discuss problems without adding information about possible solutions.

Try to identify the things the participants appreciate most about their congregation, and the ways in which the church has led them to personal growth. Identify this as the congregation's passion.

To discuss the congregation's "Best At" you will need to identify programs, services, and more that have led to growth. These will be the programs that the congregation is now offering with success. It may also be a feature of the congregation, like hospitality or community action.

It is important to be realistic. When we discuss being "best at" we are talking about potential, compared with other congregations in the community. Remember this is an internal document for developing a realistic future for the congregation.

Finally, discuss the congregation's resources. This part must cover four sections: leadership, volunteers, building, and finances. There are hints above about how to write this section. When discussing leadership, also include information about how the congregation prepares and identifies future leaders. When discussing the building, be sure to address capacity issues as well as deferred maintenance. And finally, when talking about finances, be honest about the financial capacity.

V. Vision for the Future

This is perhaps the most difficult section to write because it requires creative insight. The question it answers is: "Given our context, and our current resources, what ministry could our church be 'best at'?" At the end of chapter 3 we discussed redevelopment options; these could be part of the vision for the future of the congregation.

The vision should describe the desired congregation of the future and how it will make a difference in people's lives.

Sample Vision Statements

"X Christian Church will help the ordinary people of X lead extraordinary lives by strengthening their spiritual lives and empowering them to use that spiritual undergirding to do extraordinary things."

"Reach the Unreached. X is the Power Center in X that seeks to empower the community, city, nation and world economically, spiritually and socially by meeting their individual needs."

Following the vision statement, the ministry plan should outline how this vision will make a difference in the lives of current and future participants as well as the community. While this section is difficult, it will enable the writer to gain more clarity about this vision, and where it is leading the congregation.

Mission

There are numerous formulas for writing a mission statement. These statements work well for business, but not for the church. A church's mission statement should contain three elements: Who is the target for this ministry? What are their needs? What are you going to do about it?

A target group is the affinity group that the church is trying to reach. For existing ministries, that affinity group needs to be similar to the current congregation unless the congregation has a vision for a parallel start or restart. It is imperative that there are sufficient numbers of people in this affinity group in your context if you are to be successful. You would not want to identify seniors as your target in an area with a high cost of living index, because most seniors are leaving the area.

Many congregations get pretty upset by having to select a target for ministry. It is counterintuitive. We've been taught that Jesus loves us all. Why wouldn't the church be open to everyone? While the church *is* open to all, a congregation must pick something they can accomplish.

If you look closely at groups in congregations you will see one large affinity group no matter what their racial construct. If you take a close look even at multicultural congregations, you can also identify at least one large affinity group.

All congregations will claim some diversity. A close look will also show some common characteristics of education, economic status, and even political slant. These are difficult characteristics to traverse unless the church is engaged in a restart or parallel start. The bottom line is that "like people attract like people."

A mission statement is not for publication. It is a working understanding of the group that the congregation is attempting to attract because they can be best at meeting their needs for spiritual development.

A tacky statement would be:

"XXX Christian Church seeks to provide ministry for upper-class, white, conservative, American citizens who live in our town." While this statement is specific as to the target a congregation is trying to meet, it segregates people by class.

A good example might be:

"Primera Iglesia Cristiana's mission is to welcome first generation, Spanish-speaking immigrant families to a place that prepares them to face life in a new land, through a vibrant faith that gives them courage to face the unknown, support for their sorrows, while growing closer to Jesus Christ."

Another example is Missiongathering Christian Church in San Diego, California. The congregation uses a formative statement to describe its mission:

"Missiongathering was started by several young adults from the San Diego area who were disenchanted with the institutional church. From its initial beginnings this group of friends and spiritual seekers began to use words like *open, organic, emergent, fluid, and ever-evolving* to describe their community. They wanted to embody God's grace to the emerging/postmodern culture they were a part of. To take ancient symbols and the story of God's grace and live out what they mean for us today. This community of faith--this gathering of restless spiritual wanderers from all over San Diego County--found a safe haven for Christian spirituality as opposed to religious institutionalism. And after several years of ministry in Rancho Bernardo and La Jolla what came to be called Missiongathering began to seek the next phase in this evolving community."

Their target is "spiritual seekers". Their goal is to create an open, organic, emergent, fluid and ever-evolving community of faith. They will do that through ancient symbols and the story of God's grace. You will want to view their Web site at www.missiongathering.com. http://www.missiongathering.com/

Values

The values statement is a declaration of consistent, biblical/theological convictions that determine a congregation's priorities, influence its decisions, and drive its ministry. Most importantly, a congregation always demonstrates its values by its behavior.

Values vary from generation to generation. They also vary from community to community, and they are often unspoken. Some of these values are not biblical or theological. That is to say, the "value of hard work" ethic is not one every generation embraces. Nor is there a value that we need to have lots of meetings to make any small decision in the life of the church.

A church's value statement needs to list the things that are absolutely nonnegotiable, based on our understanding of the scriptures and theology.

Values should not be confused with practices. Practices are habits that we naturally do as a congregation. For example, weekly communion is a practice of Disciples congregations. It is not based on a belief, but is a spiritual discipline.

Finally, let me suggest that you can *see* the values held by a congregation. It is not helpful or honest to state that a congregation is committed to social justice when all it does is donate groceries to the food bank once a month. Nor is it honest to say a congregation is committed to Christian unity when the church does not participate with other congregations for anything.

Because we have high standards for these values, we need to keep the list small and simple. You cannot have twenty-three nonnegotiable values—nobody can keep track of that. We suggest five to seven. Below is a list of values some of our churches have claimed. They usually list a biblical verse that supports their value.

- Our belief in the centrality of Jesus Christ
- Our celebration of an open Lord's Table

- The ministry of all believers
- Our love of unity
- Seekers of Justice

The Biblical Story

A congregation can discover its story in the scriptures. Many new congregations identify with the story of the exodus. Since these congregations have no permanent facilities, they often wander from place to place for their early years, just like Moses and the children of Israel. When I was a new church pastor, we wandered for nine years. The only equipment that was consistent in all of our temporary places was the coffee pot and the chalice. We used to joke that the coffee pot was the "ark of the covenant" since we Seattleites love our coffee.

A biblical image is a powerful way to communicate those things that no mission, vision, or values statement could ever achieve in the imaginations of the people with whom you minister.

A number of churches have used Acts 2 as an image of what they hope their church will become. Others have used parts of the epistles that describe the followers of Christ sharing a meal and all that they have. As mentioned earlier, a congregation has used the acouunt of the man being lowered on a pallet in front of Jesus for healing, through the roof of a proud homeowner. Their image is that of a church that will let anything happen (even having its roof torn up) to bring people closer to Christ.

This story will do more to bring the values of your congregation to the forefront, and will gain unity in your actions as a congregation.

VI. *Strategies for Success*

Now that the congregation has some idea about what it wants to accomplish for the future, give some strategic ideas about how it might accomplish its vision. The strategies section is where you begin to put it all together. In this part the knowledge of your affinity group—their likes, dislikes, where they shop, what they read, and the kinds of activities they enjoy—will inform you as to how you might have success.

Four strategies must receive some reflection for the congregation to become vital. This develops a circular pattern for the ministry of the congregation.

- Reaching Strategies
- Equipping Strategies

- Empowering Strategies
- Serving Strategies

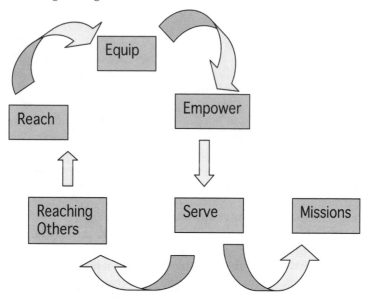

Reaching Strategies

Depending on the group you are trying to reach, you can employ numerous strategies for attracting that group. For example, if you desire to reach young families with children, you need to be aware of the things that this group is experiencing.

If you are trying to reach young families, it is important to pay attention to the mother of the household. Most likely she will decide which church the family will attend. She will consider a number of factors about that church in making her decision. Does it hold her values? Is there quality programming for her children? Will the congregation accommodate her family's scheduling issues? What will help her grow? Are there others who will help her as a parent?

Most mothers will get information for this decision from other mothers, just as they do to find a dentist. If the person sharing with her has good information about the church, and is somewhat enthusiastic about what the church is doing, it will attract her.

My wife told me about a coworker who recently chose a church home. She had been part of a smaller congregation before the birth of her children. The church, however, only offered one service at 9:00 a.m. on Sundays, and because she had twins, it was nearly impossible for her to get the children up and arrive to church by 9:00. She also had trouble with the nursery. An older volunteer whose clothes smelled of cigarette smoke staffed it. The toys were dirty, and there was no system for her gaining help if there was a problem in the nursery. There were no other young mothers in the congregation to share joys and concerns with. This mother was capable of dealing with both twins at the same time, but it took her months to learn how to do it. She did not feel comfortable leaving the babies in the nursery.

This woman eventually chose a larger congregation that offered multiple worship services and a clean, well-staffed nursery that was managed carefully to protect children from being abducted. This church also offered parenting classes for young mothers during the week. Because it offered multiple worship services, she can come to church in the middle of one service, and leave in the middle of the next one. She can come to church whenever she is ready.

While she appreciated the smaller congregation, it did nothing to accommodate her needs. Yet that very church had young families as its mission focus. If a congregation is going to have a mission focus, it must have a way for dealing with the people it hopes to attract.

This young mother learned about her new congregation from a friend who also had a small child. The friend had been a part of the bigger congregation for some time, and was prepared and encouraged to invite others to her congregation.

There are other ways to attract people if a church is intentional. Even small congregations can succeed in attracting young families, but there has to be something at the church when they arrive if the church has any hope of retaining them.

New churches rely a lot on "attraction events." These are opportunities for the general public to experience the church and its people, such as a block party where the church has inflatable toys for children to bounce on while it serves up burgers. One new church advertized a free pool party with hot dogs, and attracted more than 200 young children and parents. The event only cost about $400, and gave them a strong list of prospects.

Attraction events are only useful if you can capture names and contact information. These events are meant to allow a congregation to meet new people on neutral ground (like outside or in a park) so that people can sample the church. Attraction events are most successful if there is some gift or handout that the person will take away with them so they will remember their experience, with an invitation to the church.

If your congregation sends a newsletter or a weekly e-mail, add these prospects to the list right away, and follow up for at least two years.

The affinity group you have targeted has everything to do with the strategies you use to attract people to your church. These strategies have to be active rather than passive. Just sending out a brochure saying "We are a church for young families" is not going to achieve results. It is also suspect, particularly among the unchurched. Neutral opportunities where the congregation can begin to develop trust with people, backed by passive forms of attraction, can have great results.

Equipping Strategies

In the 1990s, a very successful new church attraction program was called "This Phone's for You." This attraction strategy involved phone banks of volunteers who called and invited thousands of people to the first worship service of a new church in their community.

We had one congregation that attracted more than 300 people to their first worship service using this approach. However, the congregation did not have any equipping strategies in place for a crowd of any size. It offered no relationships with people, no youth group, no music program, just an overworked church planter and his family trying to be a church for 300.

The next week the group was down to 150, two weeks later 90, then it bottomed out around 50 and eventually dropped to just 30. As you can imagine, this was really depressing to those who had caught the vision of this new church.

Without equipping strategies, the best attraction events will do little for your congregation. There has to be something of value for people once you get them in your congregation. People are very fickle and will not feel compelled to return if their experience with the congregation is negative. And most church visitors make their decision about returning to a church within the first fifteen minutes they are present.

Equipping strategies are the ways in which you help people mature in the faith. The majority of people are fairly uninformed about the Bible, even though 92 percent of the U.S. population has a Bible in their homes. People likely did not grow up in a church, or they may not have experienced a very effective education program in the church. Congregations need to consider a process for spiritual growth that is appropriate for both the group you are attracting and your context.

Even small congregations can offer a variety of studies for people at different stages of faith development. Not everyone can be in the same class if the church is going to grow. Teaching does not have to necessarily happen in a classroom setting. Teaching can occur in relational groups, cell groups, or other ministries engaged in other things.

In the 1960s, congregations relied heavily on men's and women's ministry groups to provide this kind of educational process. Today small groups of people with similar life issues (usually in generational groups) seem to offer the highest level of trust for meaningful conversation.

Many resources are available to congregations that will allow for a variety of experiences to enable spiritual growth. Equipping strategies also need to consider the age of participants and the life issues they face. A youth strategy will likely be pretty different from a seniors strategy.

Empowering Strategies

I looked for a church home while I was attending seminary. Since I was near a Disciples of Christ congregation, I attended their service and immediately made a startling discovery. While the people were like-minded and friendly, there was no place for me to express my gifts in that congregation.

The people in that church filled all of the spots, and had little interest in empowering others to do anything else. I visited that church again, twenty-five years later, only this time we were working through the congregation's closure. For a long time, this church did not have volunteers or leaders, and the congregation continued to decline.

It is one thing to teach others about the faith, but a congregation has to empower people to do ministry and mission. I discovered early in life that there were two kinds of youth programs: one entertained youth and the other empowered them to do mission. Empowering ministries grew. Youth who grew up in empowering ministries became congregational leaders; youth who grew up in the entertainment groups left the church afterward because it really wasn't that entertaining.

Vital congregations have strategies for individuals after they have completed their foundational learning experiences. Once you know something, it is important to get out and do something with that learning. This is far different than finding any warm body to do something. It places a value on knowing *why* you are engaged with mission, not just an assumption that people are going to do mission because they have attended a few worship services.

Empowering strategies involve identifying and recruiting future leaders and offering them leader development classes. Empowering strategies will include some requirements for leaders.

I am amazed at some of our new churches and how successful they have been in this regard. One congregation requires that leaders of the church complete a series of classes related to spiritual foundations before they can become a leader. And before they can lead they have to commit to specific spiritual practices that can be measured, such as regular church attendance, prayer, tithing, and inviting others to worship. These congregations are blessed with leaders who are deeply committed people of faith. They are also pleased as leaders to have some understanding about what is required from them.

It is important to outline a strategy of recruiting and developing future leaders for the overall mission of the congregation.

Serving Strategies

There has to be a reason for being a leader. You can have a group of highly motivated leaders who have deep spirituality, but you cannot hold them together without a purpose for ministry. Many congregations assume that once a person finds spiritual maturity they will know what to do with it. Vital congregations find ways to enable participants to engage in service to each other *and* the world.

I am always suspect of congregations that do little service outside of their faith group. Churches that spend their mission dollars only at home, or within their congregation, have missed a great deal of what being a disciple of Jesus can mean.

I have visited missionaries and mission partners overseas a number of times. I also have two sons who serve in the mission field. I can attest firsthand to the value of this work, from teaching English to Chinese minority teachers to helping children find ways to support their families in healthy ways rather than engaging in the tourist sex trade in the Dominican Republic.

The Great Commission calls us to take the Gospel to the ends of the Earth, not just to our doorsteps. I am inspired by what God is doing in these places, and congregations that do not support that work abroad discourage me.

Congregations that work together in communities are making a big difference as well. Interfaith organizations have bound themselves together in effective ways to feed, clothe, and house those who have fallen on hard times. Groups have found ways to provide effective ministry to those in prison and to people with mental health issues.

In this day and age of relatively inexpensive travel, churches can send mission groups abroad. The people who attend these trips find their lives changed forever and become tremendous supporters of global ministry.

For Disciples, Global Ministries provides numerous resources that will enable a congregation to become a "Global Mission Church." They also have resources to enable a church to take mission groups abroad. Other denominations have similar resources.

Many opportunities for mission outside of the walls of a church need the financial and volunteer support that congregations can give. Effective congregations find ways to honor the service of those in their midst who find meaningful ways of expressing their faith through service both locally and globally.

Mission is the fruit of Christian maturity. When we look to the early church in Acts, we see people serving one another with joy and faithfulness.

This final part of your ministry plan should outline how people can connect with the broader mission of the church, and how the church can prepare them to both connect new people with the church, and respond to human needs around them.

Three Sample Models

I present three models of ministry for your consideration. These are not the only models of ministry that congregations engage in, but are good examples of what a ministry plan might be like.

The Celebration-cell Model

The worship service, or "celebration," is the place where people are encouraged to become equipped and empowered leaders in this model. The attraction strategy is through outreach programs, personal invitations, and advertising. The point of attraction is to get people to the worship event, where they are challenged to become a part of a cell group (c) or ministry team (m).

The cell groups are designed to equip people with the basic disciplines and tools for faith. Some groups are focused on people very new to the faith, while others work with those who have practiced

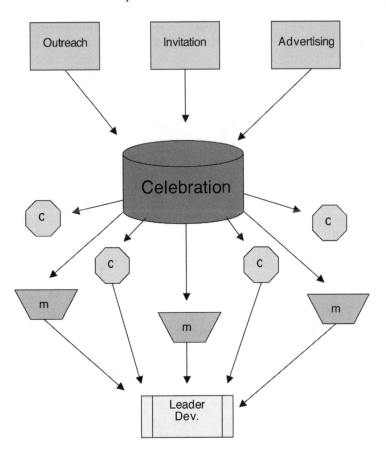

for a while. Cell groups are also designed to encourage participants to bring their friends to the celebration service. Those new people will also join their growing cell. When the cell has doubled in size, it splits. A new leader is selected and recruited for leader development. They eventually lead a new cell group, hoping that it will double in size and have to recruit a new leader and so on. Since cell group members are also engaged in the weekly celebration service, they begin to have opportunities to serve in mission groups.

Ministry groups provide ministry services. These groups include worship teams, youth leaders, teachers, and mission teams that either go abroad or serve on projects in the community. Leaders who come from the leader development class, like the cell group leaders, lead these groups. As more leaders emerge, more ministries are developed.

People are encouraged to be a part of these groups at the celebration service.

Finally, all cell groups, ministry teams, and the celebration service itself are always identifying and recruiting leaders. These future leaders attend a course on leader development where they learn "how" the church interrelates. They also have a thorough grounding in the congregation's vision, mission and values, as well as the congregation's biblical story.

The Cell-Celebration Model

In this ministry plan, the reaching out system is grounded in the cell groups. As people spend time in their small groups, they are

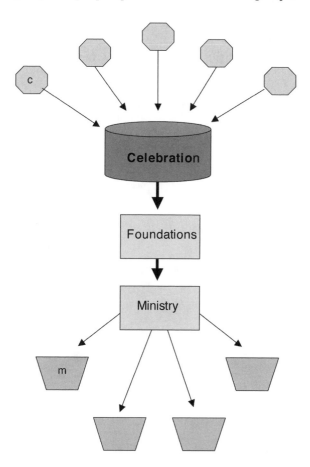

encouraged to invite others to join them in their small group rather than invite them to the worship service as in the celebration-cell model. As people develop authentic relationships in the cell, they are encouraged to become a part of the celebration and worship. This system works well with people who are suspicious of church, as it gives them a small groupin which to express their doubts, and the people bring participants to worship when the time is right.

In the celebration, people are encouraged to consider growing even more in their faith through participation in "foundations" classes. These classes start with a basic biblical overview and work their way through basic theology. The cell groups and the foundations classes serve as the equipping system.

Foundations class participants are encouraged to become leaders. Those who choose to do that enter into the ministry class series. These classes teach leader development and ground leaders in the mission, vision, and values of the church. They then become ministry team leaders, leading areas such as worship, caring networks, mission trips, etc. They may also become cell group leaders. This is their empowering *and* serving system. In this model only those who have the foundations and ministry grounding become leaders.

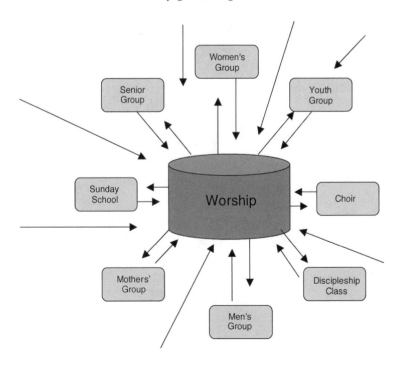

The Program Plan

When you look at this diagram you get a sense of chaos. This is the system that most congregations employ today.

The program ministry plan has no specific reaching out plan except an occasional invitation from a member, or the ad in the phone book. Some participants may first start with a group then come to the worship service. Others start in worship and perhaps join a group.

Groups spring up, some that equip and others that nurture. There is no real empowerment system that allows for leader development. People are asked to serve regardless of their understanding of the faith or grounding in the vision, mission, and values of the church, which people learn through intuition. Service opportunities are sporadi, and often include mission trips, food pantry organizing, and other volunteering.

You can begin to see the flow chart of a ministry plan and the importance of having a system for reaching, equipping, empowering, and serving.

VII. Future Organization and Management Strategy

Like a business plan, a good ministry plan will address how the congregation is going to make decisions in the future. Two principles should be considered in this section: Can decisions be made wisely and quickly with a propensity toward action? And what kind of decisions do members of the congregation want to be engaged in?

An honest assessment of most congregations today would indicate that most people do not want decisions all made by one person. Most good decisions come as a result of a number of minds looking at the same issue and adding their perspectives. Yet processes of decision making that take forever often frustate people. Small groups of wise leaders can make appropriate decisions on most matters.

Having said that, at certain times you do want to engage the entire congregation in a decision. When the vision of the church seems to indicate major shifts in how ministry is delivered, and especially when a church is considering a large capital project, people want to be involved in the decision.

Remember that 20 percent of the congregation will be providing 80 percent of the volunteering and funding. In projects that will require full cooperation and funding, you will want everyone to have a say.

This indicates that most congregations can consider a new way of leading. As discussed above, the church wants to engage most people in ministry, not decision making.

VIII. What Resources Are Needed to Accomplish This Strategy?

Most businesses and organizations fail because they do not take resources into consideration when they are launching a new initiative. Remember that resources are not just money, but volunteers and leaders, as well as the building. This section of the plan discusses the resources available in each area, with a word about what is needed for each section.

This section should include the following items:

1. Volunteer resources and challenges
2. Leadership resources and challenges
3. Facilities and challenges
4. Financial resources and challenges

Remember, we are talking about challenges and possibilities. Most congregations have far more resources than they think. This section will help the readers think in terms of abundance rather than scarcity.

IX. Congregational Process for Adoption of this Ministry Plan

People want to know how a decision is going to be made and when it will be enacted. Ministry plans raise all kinds of levels of anxiety in a congregational system. Even if the plan is iron-clad and a slam dunk for success, people will still be anxious.

Outlining the process of adopting the plan, with a timeline for enactment, is important for the future of the congregation. Every congregation has a decision-making process, but often people have differing opinions about what constitutes that process. By outlining the process you will have clarity about when the decision to move ahead will take place.

X. Appendices

The final section is where you can put newspaper articles, demographic information, charts and graphs, or basically any item that supports the ministry plan.

Turning Vision into Reality

For years, congregations have been using what is called the R.V.J. model of planning. The initials correspond to the words *Reality, Vision and Journey.* You first gain a clear sense of your *reality*, cast a *vision* for the future, and then make the *journey* toward the new vision or course set by the congregation.

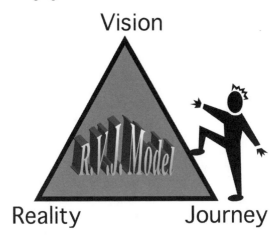

I have witnessed congregations and regional committees spend lots of time planning and casting a vision for a new future. When it comes to taking the journey, however, they are too worn out to take the first step. This is a colossal waste of time and resources.

Casting the vision should be an energizing process that propels people to get on board and work toward a new reality. If the new vision leads the congregation to making a difference in people's lives, it will likely gain support quickly, and as it unfolds it will lead the church toward a new way of being.

Nothing is more transforming than to begin to see lives changed and new relationships with Christ sprouting around you. It will be important for leaders to build momentum by celebrating even the smallest of victories, and giving the vision that God has given the church the credit for leading the congregation to a new sense of being.

In order to take a journey, you must have a destination in mind. You need resources to get you there and must have a general idea of how you will make the trip. A solid ministry plan casts a vision and describes the initial steps for that new reality. It is compelling in its style and creates energy so the church can move ahead on the same page.

I would like to end as I began, with another sailing story.

Some time ago, I was sailing a 45-foot ketch across the Strait of Georgia in British Columbia. This body of water is more than thirty miles wide and usually has high winds and currents. To sail from one side of the strait to the other requires a good chart and an accurate compass.

The night before making the crossing, I discovered that the boat was missing a key chart for navigating the strait. In addition, the two compasses on board both gave different readings. I did have two charts that I could sort of smoosh together, and I calculated the approximate heading we would have to take. The next day, I split the difference between the two compass readings and set out for the other side.

The crossing was rough at first, and then about noon the wind all but completely died out. We then did what all sailors hate to do: we fired up the iron sail (engine) and began to find our destination.

By this point we had drifted with the tide a considerable amount, and I reluctantly had to admit to the crew that I only knew approximately where we were (you never tell them you are lost). It was at this point that my binoculars became the most valuable piece of equipment on the boat. With them I was able to spot a marker as the sun set, note its number, and immediately locate it on the chart. Within an hour we were in our bay with the anchor down, eating freshly caught crab on sourdough bread.

Congregations are on a journey. At some points they become "confused" and only know approximately where they are. Some congregations have no particular destination in mind, so drifting is not a problem for them. A congregation without a specific mission does little to help people find the extraordinary life that only Christ can give.

My prayer is that you will look through your binoculars to find where you really are today. I pray that you will use the scriptures as your chart and that you discover what God has in store for your congregation and the other people whose lives depend on it.

I no longer get to make those congregational trips, but I applaud those who are doing so.

I applaud you as well as you begin to make the journey toward a new vision for your congregation. I deeply miss the life of a pastor and the many journeys I have had the privilege of making with the different churches and the saints that made them their homes.

I pray that you will discover that it is the journey, not the visioning, that is the most rewarding part of ministry planning. It is always great to know where you are going, but no journey begins without the first step. Take that step with the passion and energy that only God can give, knowing that with Christ all things are possible.

APPENDIX A

Life-cycle of a Community

John Metzger of Michigan State University wrote an article that outlines some of the ways in which community observers have defined the life-cycle. His academic paper calls on four government studies, which over time defined stages of development for communities.

While it is easy to see the systemic racism in the images of community life-cycle described by these financial writers, we need to remember they were not trying to defend racism. They were describing the life-cycles as they saw them. The racist assumptions that can grow out of these observations can serve as a reminder to us to not let statistics rule our decisions, but just to use observations as a tool in decision making.[1]

U.S. Home Owners Corp. residential security maps (1935)	U.S. Home Owners' Loan Corp. Waverly: A Study in Neighborhood Conservation (1940)
First Grade: Well-planned, homogeneous population.	First Stage: New residential construction.
Second Grade: Completely developed, stable.	Second Stage: Normal use and maintenance.
Third Grade: In transition and decline from age, obsolescence, lack of restrictions, lower household income and housing values, lack of homogeneity.	Third Stage: Age, obsolescence, structural neglect.
Fourth Grade: Final stage of decline, mostly low-income rental housing. "undesirable population."	Fourth Stage: Falling investment and rent values, neglect of maintenance, district-wide deterioration.
	Fifth Stage: Slum area with depreciated values, substandard housing, social problems.

Anatomy of a Metropolis: The Changing Distribution of People and Jobs within the New York Metropolitan Region (1959)	Real Estate Research Corporation The Dynamics of Neighborhood Change U.S. Department of Housing and Urban Development (1975)
Stage 1: Single-family residential development.	Stage 1, Healthy: Homogeneous housing and moderate to upper income, insurance and conventional financing available.
Stage 2: Transition to higher density, apartment construction.	Stage 2, Incipient Decline: Aging housing, decline in income and education level, influx of middle-income minorities, fear of racial transition.
Stage 3: Downgrading to accommodate higher density through conversion and overcrowding of existing structures, spread of ethnic and minority districts.	Stage 3—Clearly Declining: Higher density, visible deterioration, decrease in white in-movers, more minority children in schools, mostly rental housing, problems in securing insurance and financing.
Stage 4: Thinning out or shrinkage characterized by population loss and decline in housing units.	Stage 4, Accelerating Decline: Increasing vacancies, predominantly low-income and minority tenants or elderly ethnics, high unemployment, fear of crime, no insurance or institutional financing available, declining public services, absentee-owned properties.
Stage 5: Renewal through public intervention, redevelopment and replacement of obsolete housing with new multifamily apartments.	Stage 5, Abandoned: Severe dilapidation, poverty and squatters, high crime and arson, negative cash flow from buildings

APPENDIX B

Sample Ministry Plan

I. Executive Summary

For the past six months, our church has been engaged in a time of prayer and self-reflection as we listened to God about our mission as a church. To prepare this course, we engaged in prayer as a church at the start of this process with a twenty-four-hour prayer vigil. We then asked people to write reflections of their prayer time for sharing with the pastor at a later date.

During the first four months of this process, our pastor visited every household that would accept a visit. In these meetings the pastor took notes and listened carefully to the thoughts of all of our participants. We learned about the hopes and dreams of each person and how our congregation might help each other in our growth and development as Christians.

Two months ago, these preliminary notes were shared with the board, and some ideas about the future of our church began to emerge. At the direction of the board, a small team began to research our community and collect insights about the needs of different segments of our neighborhood.

Last month we asked our pastor to spend a week in retreat. At the regional retreat center, the pastor drafted this vision statement, which has been further refined by the board.

This ministry plan recognizes the significant changes in our community and envisions our church reaching out in significant ways to the Hispanic majority that now resides in our town. This is to be accomplished by the development of a new autonomous, bilingual, Hispanic congregation who will share the growing costs of operating our church, while reaching a population we cannot reach with a Disciples witness.

This ministry plan challenges our congregation to think about being a church in different ways. It reduces our church's structure, and empowers our people to be more engaged in direct mission in our community. It recognizes our strengths are in working with older adults rather than young families, and encourages us to be the best at ministering to older citizens and empty nesters by providing programs that help this segment grow.

Furthermore, this plan recognizes that all of us could benefit from a closer relationship with God in a new way. Instead of looking at our church as an organization, this plan opens up the door for us taking our discipleship more seriously. It provides avenues for spiritual growth. It also creates new ways of relating to each other, providing relational growth through new activities.

Finally, it includes a plan for attracting new participants. Using attraction events that are of interest for our new target group and targeted advertizing, we begin to put our church in front of the community once again.

It is our desire by developing this plan that FCC will do its part in the Kingdom work of all the churches in our community. We hope to gain clarity of our mission and relate in new ways to the world by joining God in that mission.

II. Congregational History

First Christian Church of Paradise was established in 1907, just as the town of Paradise was starting. The community, which is located in a rich agricultural area, was growing as new farmers established farms in the area and started raising fruit in this ideal climate.

Once the railroad established itself in our town, farming expanded, as it was now possible to get goods to the marketplace. As the town grew, so did the church. By the 1960s the church was worshiping in an older facility in downtown Paradise. This building was full of many stairs, and cramped. The church had a growing Sunday school and youth program and for a time was the center of relational life for many in the community. It was one of a handful of dominant congregations in the community at that time.

In the 1980s, the church made the bold decision to relocate to the north part of our community. Attendance had leveled out, and the church had no parking in the downtown area. The building was falling into disrepair and was expensive to maintain. At this time the church wisely relocated to what was then the northern growing edge of the community.

At that time the church averaged more than 120 in worship and offered many programs for people of all ages. The new facility was constructed with a lot of volunteer labor, and the congregation moved into the new facility without any debt. The congregation also had an excellent financial base for its ministry, and there was widespread ownership in the ministry by the congregation.

For the past twenty years the church has been experiencing significant decline. This decline increased about five years ago when the congregation requested the resignation of a pastor. Much of the decline, however, is the by-product of changing community dynamics, which were so subtle that congregational leaders didn't feel the changes.

At this time the congregation is no longer self-sustaining. It is spending assets, which were saved by a previous generation, worshiping in a building that is maintained by more than 35 percent of its budget. Due to a high level of sacrificial giving on the part of the members, the church has been able to survive. With an average worship attendance of just thirty-five, the congregation can barely keep the doors open, and the loss of a few aging members could mean greater difficulty.

As we look at our community today, we have a better understanding of the events that have led us to this spot in our history. We also see new possibilities for increasing our witness in new ways in which we can be relevant to our context. We are clear that we must adapt to these new challenges, and are grateful that we have the resources and abilities to get us to that new point.

III. Community Analysis

Paradise's economy is dominated by agriculture and service industries. Surrounded by rich farmland, orchards, and an excellent transportation system, Paradise can get its produce to market as quick as any market in the United States.

As the labor-intensive agricultural business grew, farms relied more and more on labor from migrant workers who first came to pick fruit during short seasons, then return home. It was not long before these workers began to put down roots and become citizens for Paradise.

The Hispanic population has now become the majority population in the area. Today more than 57 percent of the population is Hispanic.

The Anglo population, however, has experienced other dynamics, as in many small towns like Paradise. First, the Anglo population today has a birth rate much lower than previously and about half the rate of Hispanic families in the community. In the 1960s, church families frequently had more than more children. Today, the aging congregation has very few children and in some cases grandparents are raising the children. Overall, Anglos have had a declining birth rate in the community, and as a result is a smaller population.

Additionally, there is a tremendous migration of Anglos from Paradise to larger metropolitan areas. The members of the church attested to this in a recent conversation. Most of their children have left Paradise to start their professions and families in other communities. While the church in the '60s and '70s had a stream of generations represented in their membership, few members today have grandchildren within sixty miles.

The future will likely continue to see growth in Paradise, particularly among Hispanics. The economy is still strong; however, it is not localized in Paradise, and is controlled mostly by large companies outside the area. During the next twenty years the community's Hispanic community will grow at twice the rate of Anglos; while the community will be English dominant, it will be culturally Hispanic, specifically Mexican-American. The church's future will largely depend upon FCC's ability to adapt its ministry to these changing dynamics.

IV. Congregational Assessment

Before we can plan for the future, we need a clear picture of the condition of the congregation today. FCC is older than most vital congregations. It ialso has not grown much in the past few years, leaving us with a membership of long-term participants who are not eager to see change.

The following graph indicates the ages of our participants compared to national and community averages. This demonstrates the fact that we are missing participants in some specific groups:

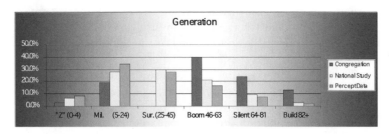

It is alarming, but 77 percent of the congregation is over forty-six years of age. Healthy congregations normally would only show about

50 percent in this category. The church is missing any participation in the Survivor category of community demographics. Generationally, the Millennials who participate are the children of the Boomers in our church and will likely leave to go to college.

When we consider the tenure of participants at FCC we see few new participants from the past few years. Today 78 percent of our congregants have participated in the church for five years or more. This is not a sustainable level of growth.

This tenure rate is the direct result of the church's inability to attract new participants. A ten-year review of our additions shows a steady decline in our ability to attract new people through baptism or transfer. While transfers may be a result of few new people moving into

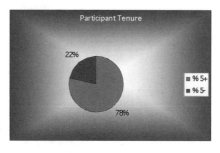

the area, the baptism rate is directly attributed to our inability to help people mature into the faith as demonstrated below.

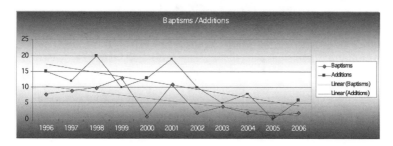

Perhaps the most glaring difference we have with our community is that our congregation is 98 percent Anglo, while the growing majority population is Hispanic. Unless our church can effectively expand its witness to this growing population it will continue to lose its potential for impact on the community.

Population by Race/Ethnicity	Anglo	African American	Hispanic	Asian	Native Am. and Other
Study Area	36%	1%	57%	4%	3%
U.S. Average	67%	12%	14%	4%	3%

The Congregation's Passion

What can this congregation be "best at"? As evidenced in interviews with congregants, FCC excels at relational work and hospitality. Numerous participants mentioned the richness of these relationships and the ways in which the church welcomed them. They also mentioned the relational programs that have enhanced their lives.

Congregants also mentioned a desire to deepen their faith. Many mentioned that while they have participated for many years in the church, they could not point to any significant learning experiences in relationship to their faith in recent years. There is a deep desire on their part to see the church equipping people in their faith practices as well as their knowledge of the scriptures. Many mentioned the fact that the congregation's two retired pastors could also help equipping others.

Resources Available for Ministry

Financial

Members of the church demonstrate a much higher than average level of giving to support the church financially. One business owner in the congregation comments that God continues to bless him as he hadsexceeded a tithe in his giving, and he has encouraged many others to exceed the tithe. While the church has great giving, the fact remains that there are not enough giving units to keep the congregation at a sustainable level.

The church is slightly out of balance in its spending. The chart below demonstrates that the church is spending more on its facilities and staff than most congregations. It does not tithe to mission as a church either.

Current Operating Budget		% of exp	% Recommended
Salary support	$64,729	53.70%	50.0%
Building/administration	$39,663	32.90%	25.0%
Program	$7,857	6.52%	15.0%
Mission	$8,300	6.89%	10.0%
TOTAL EXPENSE	$120,549		

The congregation is stressed in providing programs because it spends so much on its facilities, which are 60 percent larger than a congregation our size needs.

Leadership

The church is blessed to have several individuals who are natural leaders. These people are not only congregational leaders, but community leaders as well. In addition, a number of retired clergy who have had great education could be better utilized. However, while the church has these strong leaders, it also has done little to equip others to become leaders. A component of this plan will be to develop additional leaders in the process of extending our witness in the community.

Facilities

FCC is blessed with a twenty-five-year-old facility. The nearly 8,000 square-foot facility is located on 2.7 acres and has ample parking for growth. The sanctuary seats 120. The church is insured for $2.7 million. The facility has no debt. It does not have deferred maintenance issues. However, a new roof is likely to be needed during the next decade, and will probably cost more than $20,000.

The church site is centrally located in the community and is highly visible. It is directly across the street from Wal-Mart. The retail core around the facility is in good condition, and housing in the area is mostly well kept.

V. A Vision for the Future

Vision Statement

FCC's vision is to become the leading congregation in Paradise for meeting the spiritual and relational needs of its older citizens by engaging them in the mission of Christ for this world.

In addition, the congregation will sponsor the start of a new autonomous, Hispanic Disciples congregation in our underused facilities. This new church will be bilingual and will seek to reach out in new ways to the rapidly growing Hispanic population in our community. This church will offer programs for youth and children and expand the use of our facility. The sister congregations of FCC and the new Hispanic congregation will share in mission work in the community, and some programs.

Benefit Analysis

For Congregation Participants

Already FCC has demonstrated success with persons who are of the Boomer generation and older. Many of these people have mentioned their appreciation for how this congregation has provided them with new focus in their lives after becoming empty nesters or losing a spouse. Since 75 percent of the church is already in this age category, the church could provide programming focused on their growth rather than attempting to recreate the church of an earlier generation.

This new vision would release current participants from administrative functions and give us more time to nurture our spiritual lives. It would also get us out of the sanctuary and into the community in significant ways that would make a difference in our community with hands-on ministry.

Starting the new Hispanic faith community would enable us to have more interaction with our neighbors, crossing the racial-ethnic gaps that have kept us separate. This effort will be a witness to unity, which is a deeply held value by our congregation.

For Prospective Participants

While the number of Anglos in Paradise is declining, the number of people in the older generational groups is constant. These individuals have great skills and talents, and are starting to enjoy more leisure time as a result of retirement or of children maturing and leaving the area. These are people who may have put off their spiritual development, even though they participated in a congregation. A church that excels in a ministry focus such as outlined here could provide these individuals with a much-desired growth challenge. Additionally, many people in this group find that now that their children are grown, they have not found sufficient relational avenues with others in the community.

For the Community

Paradise has numerous social challenges. Older individuals with spirited passions could find ways to bless the community by providing tutoring for children, repairing homes for seniors, gleaning crops, etc.

Mission Statement

FCC in Paradise exists to empower older citizens in becoming engaged in God's mission on Earth. Through study, fellowship, and equipping, participants of FCC will seek to be instruments of Christ's peace for our community.

Values Statement

- FCC will stand as a symbol of Christian unity between Hispanics and Anglos in Paradise by sharing a facility and proclaiming "Somos Uno"
- Open participation for all in the Lord's Table without human judgment
- Full participation in leadership of the church with all participants
- Worship that proclaims God's unlimited ability to save
- Justice for the human family
- Recognizing we are not the only Christians, we value partnership beyond the doors of our local congregation

The Biblical Story

Therefore, if anyone is in Christ, he is a new creation; the old has gone, the new has come! All this is from God, who reconciled us to himself through Christ and gave us the ministry of reconciliation. (2 Cor. 5:17–18)

VI. Strategies for Success

Reaching Strategies

Development of attraction events for older citizens including

- Marriage enrichment seminars (Life after kids)
- Seminars on retirement planning
- Group travel experiences to neighboring cities and globally
- Golf tournament
- Cultural enrichment seminars and field trips
- Nature hikes in the Sequoia National Forest with field guides

Articles in targeted publications including:

- The County Golf newsletter
- The senior center Web site
- Targeted direct mail campaign
- Local market cable TV advertising

Networking of pastor and leaders with other organizations and service clubs.

Annual events including:

- Float in the Fourth of July parade

- Christmas bazaar
- Community picnic in the park
- Softball on Father's day

We will also network with the regional and national New Church Movement for selection, training, and coaching of the new Hispanic pastor.

Equipping Strategies

Classes related to differing levels of biblical understanding will commence in the fall. These courses will be taught in small groups that self-select. Included in these course are classes like (1) The Bible for Dummies, (2) Reading scripture like it was the first time, (3) Rediscovering Christ, (4) How do we use the Bible in our every day life?

Spiritual disciplines courses will include topics such as (1) Improving your prayer life, (2) The practice of fasting, (3) Personal finance for kingdom living.

A series of leadership classes will be offered annually by invitation only to select participants who demonstrate readiness for leadership. The pastor will teach this class, which will include preparing people for (1) Leading worship, (2) Leading a meeting, (3) Recognizing leadership in others, (4) How to empower others.

Empowering Strategies

Developing a "bottom-up" strategy for "Kingdom Now" thinking. Should a participant have an idea for ways in which our church can be better engaged in the community, we will always give permission to recruit additional support within the church. If more than 3 people show an interest in a project, the church will support it with volunteers and/or space provided it falls within the values of our church.

Serving Strategies

Each month in which there are five Sundays, we will engage in public service to our community on the fifth Sunday. After meeting for coffee at the church, groups of people will go to an appropriate place to work. Examples of this kind of service would include: building a ramp for someone who is recently disabled, cleaning up a vacant lot in our neighborhood, participating in or hosting a blood drive, passing out water for a local marathon, etc.

Additionally, each year the church will claim a mission of emphasis. This might include tutoring children, working at the food bank, or even providing baby-sitting for younger parents who need a night off.

VII. Future Organization and Management Strategy

Conversations with members made it apparent that we have way more structure and meetings than needed to operate our church. We will reduce the number of board members to just four people, plus the pastor, who will meet four times per year to review the business and finances of the church. This will be known now as the "cabinet."

There will no longer be standing committees, except for the Elders, who will meet briefly each month to share assignments for pastoral care of the congregation, specifically the shut-ins.

Because all programs are perpetuated from membership, the pastor becomes the coordinator of programs, unless the program is of a nature that it might conflict with the congregation's values. In those cases the cabinet will confirm the program suggestions.

VIII. What resources are needed to accomplish the strategy?

The congregation will need to reallocate current program funds to create a fund for new programs and attraction events. However, most programs will be self-funded and most likely not require additional costs.

Leadership for both lay and clergy will require some significant training initially. The congregation will ask the regional office to provide leadership for a planning retreat in early May, at which time the vision will be flushed out with more details.

IX. Congregational Process for Adoption of this Ministry Plan

The ministry plan will be introduced to the congregation at the annual meeting in January. The written document will be distributed to the congregation, and a series of home meetings will be announced. It is hoped that at least 60 percent of the congregation will sign up for these meetings.

The home meetings will begin in February. As part of the discussion, each home group will be invited to dream up programs that they could initiate. Each group will also be asked to practice several new prayer disciplines during the week between meetings.

The second and final meeting will be to list ideas and inspirations that come from the groups.

In March, there will be another meeting of the congregation to formally adopt this ministry plan.

Once thye plan is adopted, a timeline will be established for implementing programs as well as the launch of the new Hispanic ministry by September.

X. Conclusion

FCC no longer can serve the community as it did at one time. Today more than seventy congregations in our community seek to serve the same small group of individuals. By being the best at serving those whom we already serve well, we believe we can grow again.

In addition, it is time for all of us to once again ignite that "first love" that we once felt about Christ. To be transformed as a congregation, we must once again look at Jesus as if it is our first time. We must once again look at the issues that surround our community, and be a sign of wholeness in our broken world.

We can no longer pretend that the large Hispanic community in Paradise does not exist, or that every person of Spanish-speaking descent is Catholic. A large population of unchurched people of all races lives in our community.

It is time that FCC steps up to the challenge of being a church full of passionate Disciples who are impatient with the human condition, rather than a membership organization that cares only for itself.

While this plan does not guarantee numeric growth, we know that all of us who call FCC our church home will grow personally in this new model of being a church. When Jesus met with his disciples that last time, he was clear about our mission as a church, to *go* and make disciples. May God inspire us again to be agents for change in the world.

We, the members of this church board, forward this plan to the congregation for discussion. We endorse it for adoption with the sure and certain hope that we are called to rise to the challenges of this time we face today.

Notes

Introduction

[1]See Michael and Diane Porter, "How Binoculars Work," Bird Watching.com, available at: http://birdwatching.com.

[2]William Sloane Coffin, *Credo* (Lousiville: Westminster John Knox Press, 2005).

[3]Mark Lau Branson, *Memories, Hopes, and Conversations: Appreciative Inquiry and Congregational Change* (Danbury, Conn.: Alban Institute, 2004).

[4]Ibid.

Chapter 1: A Macro Lens of Doing Church Today

[1]See Michael and Diane Porter, "How Binoculars Work," Bird Watching.com, available at: http://birdwatching.com.

[2]Michael W. Foss, *Power Surge: Six Marks of Discipleship for a Changing Church* (Minneapolis: Fortress Press, 2000).

[3]George Barna, *What Americans Believe: An Annual Survey of Values and Religious Views in the United States* (New York: Regal Books, 1991).

[4]David T. Olson & Craig Groeschel, *The American Church in Crisis: Groundbreaking Research Based on a National Database of over 200,000 Churches* (Grand Rapids: Zondervan, 2008).

[5]Ibid.

[6]Gallup: 2006 to 2008, available at: http://gallup.com/poll/content/?c=7759.

[7]Information available at Stats Extracts: http://stats.oecd.org/Index.aspx?DataSetCode=ANHRS.

[8]Norman Herr, "The Sourcebook for Teaching Science," *Television and Health* (July 31, 2008), available at: http://www.csun.edu/science/health/docs/tv&health.html#tv_stats.

[9]Larry Copeland, "As Communities begin earlier, new daily routines emerge," *USA Today,* (Sept. 12, 2007).

[10]U.S. Census Bureau, available at: http://www.census.gov/.

[11]Susan J. Wells, "Job tenure statistics yield some surprises," *The Journal Record* (Oklahoma City), (August 24, 1998), available at: http://findarticles.com/p/articles/mi_qn4182/is_19980824/ai_n10122090/.

[12]Stephen Compton, *Rekindling the Mainline* (Bethesda, Md.: Alban Institute, 2003).

[13]Wade C. Roof and William McKinney, *America Mainline Religion: Its Changing Shape of the Religious Establishment* (Herndon, Va.: New York: Rutgers UP, 1987).

[14]U.S. Census Bureau, available at: http://www.census.gov/

[15]Ibid.

[16]Thomas L. Friedman, *The World Is Flat: A Brief History of the Twenty-First Century* (New York: Farrar, Straus & Giroux, 2006).

[17]*Hoosier* is a popular term used by residents of Indiana to describe themselves.

[18]Ed Stetzer and David Putman, *Breaking the Missional Code: Your Church Can Become a Missionary in Your Community* (New York: B&H Group, 2006).

[19]Jorge Ramos, *The Latino Wave: How Hispanics Are Transforming Politics in America* (New York: Rayo, 2005).

[20]U.S. Census Bureau, available at: http://www.census.gov/.

[21]Lynne C. Lancaster and David Stillman, *When Generations Collide: Who They Are, Why They Clash, How to Solve the Generational Puzzle at Work* (New York: HarperCollins, 2003).

[22]U.S. Census Bureau, available at: http://www.census.gov/.

[23]Foss, *Power Surge.*

[24]Study Abroad, available at: http://www.vistawide.com/studyabroad/study_ statistics.htm.

[25]From Mindfully.org, available at: http://www.mindfully.org/Sustainability/ Americans-Consume-24percent.htm.

[26]"Church Attendance on Decline," *Christian Century* (September 11, 1996), available at: http://findarticles.com/p/articles/mi_m1058/is_n26_v113/ai_18720688/? tag=content;col1.

[27]Stanley M. Hauerwas and William H. Willimon, *Resident Aliens: Life in the Christian Colony* (New York: Abingdon Press, 1989).

[28]"Church Attendance on Decline."

Chapter 2: Exegete Your Community

[1]See the New Direction Christian Church site at http://www.n2newdirection. org/.

[2]Missioninsite Mosaic Guide ©2008 Decisioninsite, LLC and MissionInsite, LLC. To learn more about Mosaic, go to www.missioninsite.com, and click the resource button. (New Beginnings© congregations get this kind of analysis with their reports. Other congregations may wish to subscribe to MissionInsite for their own analysis.)

[3]"Redlining: Definition," at About.com:Home Buying/Selling, available at: http:// homebuying.about.com/od/glossaryqr/g/053107Redlining.htm.

[4]John T. Metzger, "Planned Abadonment: The Neighborhood Life-cycle Theory and National Urban Policy," *Housing Policy Debate* 11 (2000).

[5]U.S. Census Bureau, available at: http://www.census.gov/.

[6]Lyle Schaller is often considered the "dean of church consultants." He has written numerous books on his observations of congregations and church life over the past forty years.

[7]U.S. Census, available at: http://www.census.gov/.

[8]George W. Bullard Jr., *Pursuing the Full Kingdom Potential of Your Congregation* (St. Louis: Chalice Press, 2006).

[9]Child Trends Data Bank, available at: http://www.childtrendsdatabank.org/ archivepgs/79.htm.

[10]Martin Luther King, "Questions and Answers of his 1963 Western Michigan University speech," available at: http://www.wmich.edu/library/archives/mlk/q-a. html.

[11]"Families are Changing," *USA Today* (Nov. 24, 1999).

[12]U.S. Census, available at: http://www.census.gov/.

[13]Centers for Disease Control and Prevention, "Cohabitation, Marriage, Divorce, and Remarriage in the U.S," Vital Health and Statistics Series 23, number 22, Department of Health and Human Services, 2002.

[14]U.S. Census, 2000.

[15]U.S. Census Bureau, "America's Families and Living Arrangements," available at: http://www.census.gov/.

[16]National Center for Health Statistics, 2000 data, available at: http://www.cdc. gov/nchs/.

[17]U.S. Census, available at: http://www.census.gov/.

[18]American Council on Education statistics, available at: http://www.acenet.edu/ AM/Template.cfm?Section=Home.

[19]From University of Chicago Library, available at: www.lib.uchicago.edu/e/su/maps/neighborhoodnote2000.html.

Chapter 3: Assessing Congregational Readiness

[1]Jim Griffith and Bill Easum, *Ten Most Common Mistakes Made by New Church Starts* (St. Louis: Chalice Press, 2008).

[2]See http://www.enotes.com/small-business-encyclopedia/organizational-life-cycle.

[3]Ibid.

[4]C. Otto. Scharmer, *Theory U: Leading from the Future as It Emerges* (San Francisco: Berrett-Koehler, 2009).

[5]Alice Mann, *Raising the Roof: The Pastoral-to-Program Size Transition* (Danbury, Conn.: Alban Institute, 2001).

[6]Israel Galindo, *The Hidden Lives of Congregations : Understanding Church Dynamics* (Danbury, Conn.: Alban Institute, 2004).

[7]Malcolm Gladwell, *The Tipping Point: How Little Things Can Make a Big Difference* (New York: Back Bay, 2002).

[8]Kennon L. Callahan and Ian B. Tanner, *Twelve Keys to an Effective Church: Strategic Planning Mission* (San Francisco: Jossey-Bass, 1997).

[9]Penny Edgell Becker, *Congregations in Conflict: Cultural Models of Local Religious Life* (San Francisco: Harper & Row, 1984).

[10]Gladwell, *Tipping Point.*

[11]Ibid.

[12]Gilbert R. Rendle illustrates how difficult is to achieve consensus in the many stories contained in *Leading Change in the Congregation: Spiritual and Organizational Tools for Leaders* (Danbury, Conn.: Alban Institute, 1998).

[13]Gladwell illustrates this throughout *Tipping Point.*

[14]From a personal conversation with Hamm.

[15]See www.link2lead.com.

[16]John Holt, *How Children Fail* (New York: Da Capo, 1995).

Chapter 4: Good to Great Congregations

[1]Jim Collins, *Good to Great: Why Some Companies Make the Leap...And Others Don't* (New York: HarperCollins, 2001).

[2]Jim Collins, *Good to Great and the Social Sectors: Why Business Thinking Is Not the Answer* (New York: Jim Collins, 2005).

[3]William M. Easum, *The Complete Ministry Audit: How to Measure 20 Principles for Growth* (New York: Abingdon Press, 1996).

[4]Ibid.

[5]Frederick Buechner, *The Longing for Home: Reflections at Midlife* (New York: Harper San Francisco, 1996).

[6]Collins, *Good to Great.*

[7]Take a quick peek in the ministry planning section to see a way of measuring your current use of volunteers.

[8]Jim Griffith and Bill Easum, *Ten Most Common Mistakes Made by New Church Starts* (St. Louis: Chalice Press, 2008).

[9]Lyle E. Schaller, *The Small Church Is Different* (Nashville: Abingdon Press, 1982).

Chapter 5: Called for a Particular Purpose

[1]Stephen Covey, *The 7 Habits of Highly Effective People* (New York: Free Press, 2004).

[2]George A. Buttrick et al. *The Interpreter's Dictionary of the Bible* (New York: Abingdon Press, 1962).

[3]Martha Grace Reese, *Unbinding the Gospel*, 2d ed. (St. Louis: Chalice Press, 2008); *Unbinding Your Church* (St. Louis: Chalice Press, 2008); *Unbinding Your Heart* (St. Louis: Chalice Press, 2008); *Unbinding Your Soul* (St. Louis: Chalice Press, 2009).

[4]C. Otto. Scharmer, *Theory U: Leading from the Future as It Emerges* (San Francisco: Berrett-Koehler, 2009).

[5]Israel Galindo, *The Hidden Lives of Congregations: Understanding Church Dynamics* (Danbury, Conn.: Alban Institute, 2004).

[6]Ibid.

[7]Ibid.

[8]Wallace B. Clift, *Jung and Christianity: The Challenge of Reconciliation* (New York: Crossroad Classic, 1983).

[9]See http://en.wikipedia.org/wiki/Volition_(psychology).

[10]James W. Fowler, *Stages of Faith: The Psychology of Human Development* (New York: Harper San Francisco, 1995).

Chapter 6: Writing a Ministry Plan

[1]Thomas J. Peters, and Robert H. Waterman, *In Search of Excellence: Lessons from America's Best-Run Companies* (New York: HarperCollins, 2004).

[2]Ibid.

Appendix A: Life-cycle of a Community

[1]John T. Metzger, "Planned Abandonment: The Neighborhood Life-cycle Theory and National Urban Policy," *Housing Policy Debate* 11 (2000).

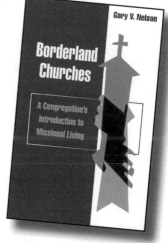

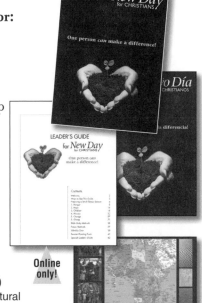